LOOPY MANGO KNITTING

LOOPY MANGO KNITTING

34 FASHIONABLE PIECES YOU CAN MAKE IN A DAY

OEJONG KIM

Abrams, New York

CONTENTS

INTRODUCTION

LOOPY MANGO

I was born in Korea and went to college in Japan. After graduating from Tokyo University of Foreign Studies, I worked as an interpreter and later opened a Korean fusion restaurant in Nagoya, Japan. Then I moved to New York and worked for a corporate housing company, and it was at that time I found a crochet hook in my suitcase. To this day, I don't know how that crochet hook got there. This was way back in 2004—before YouTube had a video tutorial for everything. While I had learned to knit and to crochet from my mom as a child, I was never very interested in it. I wanted to learn how to crochet again, so I went to Barnes & Noble, bought a book, and taught myself. I was hooked (pun intended) instantly and every day it was becoming more and more difficult to keep going back to work; all I wanted to do was crochet. I finally took a vacation and never went back.

Around that same time, I met my future business partner—Anna—in a fabric painting workshop at the Fashion Institute of Technology (FIT). It turned out Anna had learned how to crochet from her mother and how to knit from her grandmother while growing up in the former Soviet Union. She had moved to New York after quitting her software engineering job at Expedia to become an artist. After we met at FIT, she asked me to pose for a portrait. I brought my crocheting with me and crocheted a shawl while she was sketching. I was using this beautiful deep purple mohair yarn, and she was so fascinated by it that she asked me to show her how to crochet again. I took her to some yarn stores, and the next thing you know she too was so hooked that she dropped out of her graduate school program. It was then that we decided to open a boutique in the East Village. We called it Loopy Mango.

The original Loopy Mango store went through many iterations during its ten-year life span. Our original idea was to sell my crocheted creations and Anna's artwork. We quickly learned that it wasn't enough to keep the store afloat and added ready-to-wear pieces and accessories from independent designers from all over the world. When we moved our store to SoHo in 2010, we expanded into gifts, homeware, and textiles and became a lifestyle boutique. My lifestyle has always included yarn and knitting, and so I persuaded Anna to throw that in too! We added some of my favorite yarn brands to our store assortment and had a great response from customers. But I still wasn't satisfied.

We both loved to knit and crochet and wanted to share our love of this ancient craft with everyone. But learning to knit can be very frustrating unless you use the right tools and materials. We couldn't find the tools and materials that we were dreaming about, so we started making our own yarn and needles. We were then able to teach someone how to knit in just one to two hours—and not to simply learn the stitches, but to have a completed project at the end. A hat, a scarf, a cowl, even a blanket. It was such a joy watching our students proudly put on their first hat or scarf after a class. At the end of the day, that's all that really matters to us: making a product that makes people happy.

ABOUT THIS BOOK

Every knitting pattern in this book was designed with the beginner in mind. I believe in breaking down knitting techniques into simple steps that any novice can follow. Anyone can start with a scarf or a hat (or even a blanket) and progress to a sweater or a cardigan. Once you master the basic stitches, you can make almost anything. There is so much you can do with very simple stitches—good design doesn't necessarily mean complicated. But most importantly, knitting is fun, and I want you to enjoy both learning to knit and your finished projects.

When I first started knitting, the books I came across seemed too complicated, with many projects that were too time consuming to complete. I wanted to make something simple, fast, and modern.

When I design, I put all the aspects—material, color, texture, weight—together and edit them. I like to create designs that I can wear and enjoy every day, and that will last forever. Creating modern, stylish-yet-classic pieces is most important to me. When I think about Loopy Mango knitters I think about simple, effortless, classic, modern women and men. And of course, the pieces have to knit up fast!

A FEW THINGS TO KEEP IN MIND ABOUT THIS BOOK

Is it more difficult for a beginner to knit with big yarn and knitting needles? Absolutely not! Quite the opposite—the bigger the needles and the thicker the yarn, the easier and faster it is to learn how to knit. Every stitch you make is magnified. You can clearly see what you are doing, and there are a lot fewer chances to make mistakes.

The patterns are divided into different skill level sections: Absolute Beginner, Beginner, and Intermediate.

 ABSOLUTE BEGINNER: No experience of any kind is necessary. Projects only use cast on, knit stitch, and cast off, all of which are explained and illustrated in the "Knitting Basics" and "Stitches & Techniques" sections (see pages 29 and 147).

 BEGINNER: These projects require the ability to do basic knitting techniques, such as cast on, knit stitch, purl stitch, increase, decrease, and cast off.

 INTERMEDIATE: For these projects, proficiency of all beginner level techniques is needed, as well as the shaping of garments and more involved finishing techniques.

If you have never tried knitting before but always wanted to, this book is for you. We will teach you the building blocks of knitting, and your first project can be a beautiful chunky scarf or a hat that will only take you a few hours to complete. Once you complete your first project or two, you are no longer at the Absolute Beginner level and you can move on to the Beginner projects.

If you have knitted in the past and want to get back into it but feel a bit nervous, this book is for you. Knitting is like riding a bicycle—because of muscle memory, your hands will remember how to do the stitches even if you think your brain doesn't remember anymore. And once you pick up those knitting needles again, you won't want to put them down.

If you are an experienced knitter and like the aesthetic of simple, modern design, this book is for you.

Loopy Mango will always be a place for fun, easy-to-make, incredibly stylish pieces that you'll want to keep in your closet forever. Our designs are full of pieces we love, using materials and a process that we're proud of and excited to share.

TOOLS & MATERIALS

YARN

I like to use the best materials in my work, and I encourage even beginner knitters to do the same. It doesn't have to be expensive, but it has to be made with good-quality, natural fibers—wool, cotton, mohair. Big Loop was the first yarn we developed back in 2011. It is very thick and luxurious but very durable because it has a cotton core inside to give it additional strength. We make it at our own mill in Key Largo, Florida. Our other yarns—Merino No. 5, Mohair So Soft, and Big Cotton—are all made at small mills in Italy, exclusively for Loopy Mango.

In this book, we used three different yarns that are designed and made by Loopy Mango. The yarns are Big Loop, Merino No. 5, and Mohair So Soft. Big Loop and Merino No. 5 are made with 100% merino wool fiber. Mohair So Soft is made with 47% superkid mohair and 53% superfine merino wool. We prefer merino to regular wool because it is much softer and feels great on sensitive skin. Merino wool comes from merino sheep—fiber from this breed of sheep is very soft and has a low micron count; micron count in yarn refers to the diameter of an individual strand of fiber. There are different grades of merino too. That is why some merino wool will feel softer than others.

However, you can substitute any regular chunky wool of your choice for the projects in this book—just make sure to match the gauge in the pattern and read the tip section below about choosing substitute yarns—and you will have a similar look.

In our experience, thicker yarn and large-size knitting needles are the best to learn on. It is much easier to understand the techniques and see what you are doing, not to mention that everything goes much quicker. In fact, the reason many people give up knitting in the first place is because they were taught using thin yarn and thin needles, which results in frequent mistakes, dropped stitches, and slow progress. Once you get the hang of the basics you can go experiment with thinner yarns and smaller needles, and you'll likely have a much more enjoyable experience because everything will make a lot more sense.

PURCHASING YARN

Purchasing yarn for a project is a very important step. If you are on the fence between six or seven balls, it is always better to buy more. If you run out of yarn, you may not be able to buy an additional ball in the same dye lot.

So, what is a dye lot? All yarn in the same dye lot is guaranteed to have an exact color match. Yarns can have the same color name, but different dye lots will have slight variations in color. This happens because the yarns in the different lots are dyed in different batches, and many factors can affect how the color comes out—the base color of the natural undyed wool, the temperature of water, the amount of dye. Dye lot is usually shown in a number printed on the yarn label.

YARN LABELS

Always save at least one yarn label until you are finished with a project so that you will know the brand, color, and dye lot in case you need to buy more yarn. Other useful information on yarn labels includes the care instructions and the fiber content.

Even when you are finished with the project, we recommend keeping a label and a small swatch of yarn to use for future reference. To help keep your projects organized, tape the label and swatch into a notebook and write any notes about the project while it is still fresh in your memory, in case you want to make the same garment in the future. Or take a picture and save your notes in an electronic format—this way you don't have to worry about losing them.

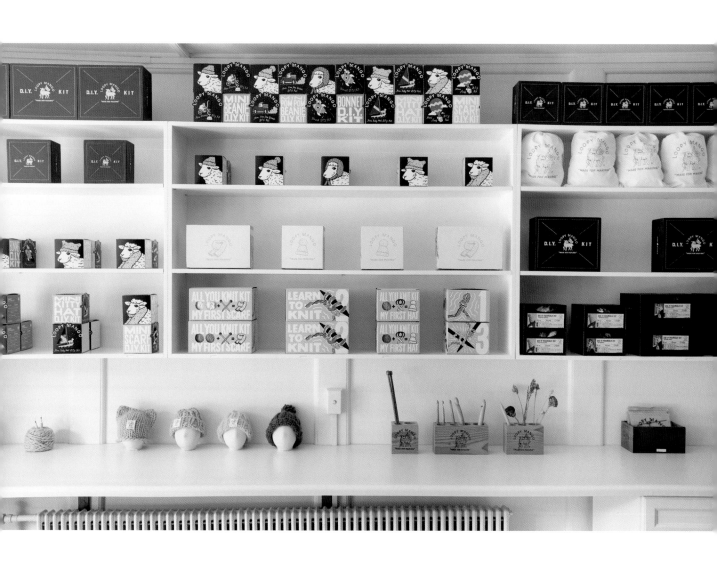

HOW TO SUBSTITUTE YARNS

If you want to substitute one yarn for another, make sure you get the same yardage—see below for how to make the calculations. Additionally, you will want to choose a yarn that is in the same weight category, e.g., bulky to bulky, as the yarn recommended in your pattern. Next, you will want to make a gauge swatch with the new yarn and check the gauge carefully, using whatever size needle is needed to obtain the gauge in the pattern.

So, for example, if the project requires 4 balls of Merino No. 5, this calculates out to 74 yards per ball, so 74 yards × 4 balls (or number needed for project) = 296 yards total. Next, divide the total number of yards needed for your pattern by the number of yards in each skein of your substitute yarn. Let's assume your substitute yarn is of the same weight and has 60 yards per ball. Calculate as follows: 296 yards needed for your pattern ÷ 60 yards per ball = 4.93 balls. Round up to 5 for the closest whole number of balls, and that is how many balls of substitute yarn you will need to buy.

GARMENT CARE

When caring for your knitted garment, always read the yarn label. You can also experiment with a small knitted swatch of your yarn and different detergents or washing processes. In general, wool is prone to felting (shrinking) when exposed to heat or agitation. We recommend dry cleaning or hand-washing wool garments in cold water and laying them flat to dry in order to avoid shrinking. Hundred-percent wool is known to be self-cleaning, so unless your garment gets soiled, it is sufficient to just air it out—leave it outside overnight and it will smell fresh again.

Knitwear is also prone to stretching, so never store your garment by hanging it; keep the item folded on a shelf. Beware of moths as they are attracted to wool fibers. Dried lavender is a great natural moth repellent.

Chunky natural fibers can start to develop pills. The best way to deal with pills is to simply cut them off with a pair of scissors. Large-bladed scissors work best because you can get multiple pills all at once, and your garment will look like new again.

NEEDLES & NOTIONS

KNITTING NEEDLES

Knitting needles are available in various materials such as wood, plastic, or metal, each having a different feel, finish, and weight. Metal needles are very smooth and can be too slippery for a beginner, but a more advanced knitter might prefer them because the yarn slides off easier, allowing for faster knitting. Some people prefer the feel of natural wood in their hands as compared to man-made materials. In general, we recommend wood or plastic needles for beginners.

Needles are either straight or circular and come in a range of sizes and lengths. Straight, single-pointed needles have a point on one end and a knob on the other end and come in pairs. Circular needles are a pair of pointed shorter needles connected on opposite ends by a flexible cable.

There are two sizes associated with knitting needles: the diameter of the thickest part of the needle; and the length of the needle from one tip to the other tip for circular needles, and from the point to the knob for straight needles.

Note: Different countries use different conventions for measuring knitting needles. For example, a US size 15 knitting needle measures 10 mm in diameter. When purchasing knitting needles in another country, make sure that you are purchasing the right size for your yarn or project.

NOTIONS

Notions are accessories that are useful for knitting projects. Here are some notions to consider having on hand to start: a measuring tape, a large tapestry needle for joining seams, and a few stitch markers. Other things to add as you progress are cable needles, a felting needle and mat, and crochet hooks.

Buttons and other hardware, such as rings or hooks, can be bought as needed for specific projects.

DIY KITS

A kit is great for a beginner, as it usually has everything you need to complete a project. Typically, a DIY kit will include yarn, knitting needles, and instructions, so if you prefer to buy all the necessary items in one package, you can! Kits are worth sourcing out, depending on which materials you need, but are not necessary for any of the projects in this book. Read more about our Loopy Mango kits in the Resources section (see page 184).

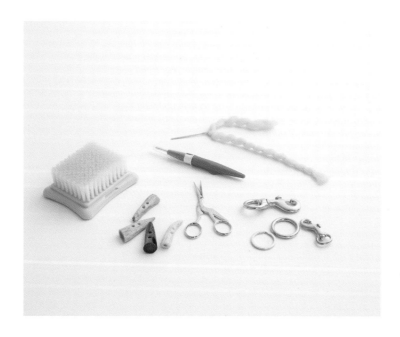

MY FIRST SCARF

STEP 1   MAKE SLIP KNOT (COUNT IT AS YOUR FIRST STITCH)

STEP 2   CAST ON 11 MORE STITCHES (TOTAL OF 12 INCLUDING SLIP KNOT)

STEP 3   KNIT 12 STITCHES

STEP 4   REPEAT STEP 3 UNTIL YOU HAVE ABOUT 24 90 CM OF YARN LEFT OVER

STEP 5   CAST OFF

STEP 6   WEAVE IN ENDS

STEP 7   ENJOY YOUR NEW SCARF AND SHARE WITH FRIENDS #LOOPYMANGO

WATCH VIDEO LESSONS
LOOPYMANGO.COM

ALL YOU KNIT KIT
MY FIRST SCARF

KNITTING BASICS

HOW TO
MAKE A SLIP
KNOT

Most knitting projects start with
a slip knot.

A. Make a loop.

B. Pull the longer end of yarn
(working yarn) through that loop
and insert one of the knitting
needles through the slip knot.

C. Tighten by pulling the
working yarn (don't pull too
tightly—make sure it fits loosely
on the needle).

A

B

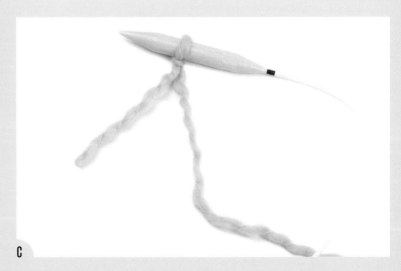

C

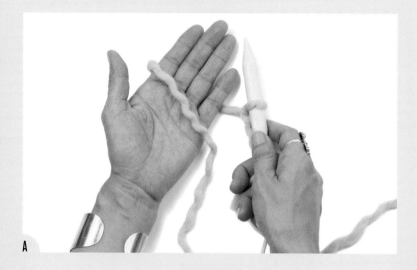

HOW TO CAST ON

Casting on is the process of getting that first row or round of stitches onto your needle. There are numerous ways to cast on. The Backward Loop is the easiest, and we recommend it for all of the projects in this book (except for the Her Beanie [see page 57] where the Knitted Cast-On is better). Different cast-on methods give you different edges, and you can experiment with other methods as you become a more experienced knitter.

Backward Loop Cast-On

Make a slip knot and hold the needle with your right hand.

A Wrap the yarn around your left hand.

B Pick up the yarn with the same needle.

C Adjust (tighten—but don't pull too tightly).

Knitted Cast-On

Make a slip knot on the end of one needle, leaving a tail.

A Insert the needle through the stitch from front to back.

B Wrap the yarn around the needle toward you (yarn over).

C Pull the yarn through the stitch.

D Twist the stitch.

E Put it back onto the left-hand needle.

F Pull the right needle out.

Tip: Make sure to always twist the stitch in the same direction.

A

B

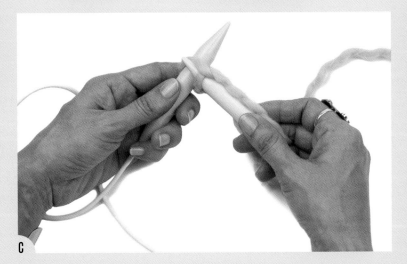

C

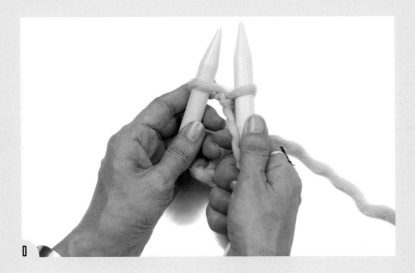

D

E

F

HOW TO MAKE A KNIT STITCH

The Knit Stitch is the most important and fundamental stitch in knitting. You can make many garments just by knitting this stitch alone. It is a simple, four-step process. We highly encourage you to repeat these steps in your head until they become second nature and you develop muscle memory. If you have ever knitted in the past, even as a child many years ago, you will discover that when you pick up knitting needles again your brain may not remember how knitting works, but your hands somehow know how to do it. It's like riding a bicycle!

A Insert the needle through the loop from front to back.

B Wrap the yarn around the right-hand needle (toward you)—yarn over.

C Pull the yarn through the loop.

D Take the stitch off the left needle.

Tip: Keep needles perpendicular to each other (at a 90-degree angle).

A

B

C

D

HOW TO MAKE A PURL STITCH

Make sure the yarn is to the front of the needle.

A Insert the needle through the loop from back to front.

B Wrap the yarn around the right-hand needle (toward you)—yarn over.

C Push the yarn out through the loop, away from you.

D Take the stitch off the left needle.

KNITTING
BASICS

HOW TO BIND OFF

If you don't bind off the stitches after knitting the last row, when you take the needle out and pull on the yarn, your entire project will unravel. You need to secure the stitches by binding off the last row of stitches one by one to prevent the piece from unraveling. The terms "bind off" and "cast off" are interchangeable and have the same meaning.

Knit one stitch.

A   Knit the next stitch. You now have two knitted stitches on the right-hand needle.

B/C Pull the yarn from the first stitch to the left, over the second stitch.

D   Push it off the left-hand needle.

E   You now have only one stitch on the right-hand needle.

Repeat steps A–E until there are no more stitches on the left-hand needle and only one stitch on the right-hand needle.

Cut the yarn, leaving a tail 2 to 3 inches (5 to 7.5 cm) long.

Remove the remaining stitch from the needle and thread the tail end through the loop to secure it.

A

B

C

KNITTING ABBREVIATIONS

C4B (Cable 4 Back) = Slip next 2 stitches onto cable needle and hold at back of work, knit next 2 stitches from left-hand needle, then knit stitches from cable needle

C4F (Cable 4 Front) = Slip next 2 stitches onto cable needle and hold at front of work, knit next 2 stitches from left-hand needle, then knit stitches from cable needle

ch = chain stitch in crocheting

K1 = Knit 1 stitch

K1B = Knit 1 Below (used in Fisherman Rib stitch)

K2TOG = Knit 2 stitches together (decrease)

KFB = Increase by knitting through front and back of the stitch

K = knit

M1 = Increase by making 1 stitch

ML = Make Loop stitch

P1 = Purl 1 stitch

P1B = Purl 1 Below (used in Fisherman Rib stitch)

P3TOG = Purl 3 stitches together (decrease)

P = purl

pm = place marker

rep = repeat

rnd = round

SL = slip stitch

st = stitch

St st = Stockinette stitch

T3B (Twist 3 Back) = Slip next stitch onto cable needle and hold at back of work, knit next 2 stitches from left-hand needle, then purl stitch from cable needle

T3F (Twist 3 Front) = Slip next 2 stitches onto cable needle and hold at front of work, purl next stitch from left-hand needle then knit stitches from cable needle

yo = yarn over

ABSOLUTE

BEGINNER

8 × 60 inches
(20 × 152 cm)

LEVEL OF EXPERIENCE

Absolute Beginner (time to
complete: 2 to 4 hours)

MATERIALS

Merino No. 5 by Loopy
Mango, 5.3 ounce
(150 g) balls each
74 yards (68 m)

2 balls in Jungle

US size 19 (15 mm) circular
needles, at least
16 inches (40 cm) long
or US size 19 (15 mm)
straight needles, at least
13 inches (33 cm) long

GAUGE

10 sts = 6½ inches
(16.5 cm) in garter stitch

10 rows = 3½ inches
(9 cm) in garter stitch

This scarf is one of the simplest projects in this book. If you already know how to knit, you can easily make this scarf in two to three hours. Even if you don't know how to knit, you can still make it in only two to four hours. The scarf is worked flat using only garter stitch, and you can use either straight or circular needles. Garter stitch is one of the most versatile stitches in all of knitting. It is simple yet yields a very modern look. This is a great first project for any beginner!

With either circular or straight needles,
cast on 12 sts.

ROW 1: K12.

Continue in knit st until scarf is
60 inches (152 cm) long. Make sure
you have at least 36 inches (30 cm)
of yarn left over for binding off.

Bind off.

Finishing

See finishing instructions on page 173.

MY
FIRST
SCARF

MY
FIRST
HAT

9 × 9 inches (23 × 23 cm)

Absolute Beginner (time to complete: 1 to 2 hours)

Merino No. 5 by Loopy Mango, 5.3 ounce (150 g) balls each 74 yards (68 m)

1 ball in Polar Bear

US size 19 (15 mm) circular needles, 16 inches (40 cm) or 20 inches (50 cm) long

4 sts = 3 inches (7.5 cm)

4 rows = 2 inches (5 cm)

This is the easiest hat in the book—yes, even easier than the Helsinki Hat (see page 46)—and you can add a pompom to it! If you know how to knit, it will take you no more than one hour. If you don't know how to knit, you should be able to do it in about two hours. The hat uses knit stitch only and is knit in the round. Don't be afraid of knitting in the round, even if you have never done it. Once you are past connecting your first round (making sure not to twist the stitches; see page 157), it will be a breeze.

Cast on 26 sts.

Join yarn to work in the rnd, being careful not to twist sts. Place marker.

Rnd 1 to 25: K26.

Cut the yarn, leaving about 15 inches (38 cm). Pull the yarn end through every st on the needle, remove the needle, then pull on the end to tighten up the top of the hat. Secure and fasten off.

Finishing

POMPOM (SEE ALSO PAGE 172)
Cut a piece of cardboard to measure 3 × 5 inches (7.5 × 13 cm).

Wrap remaining yarn around the cardboard 30 to 35 times, using short end of cardboard for a smaller pompom or long end of cardboard for a bigger pompom.

Carefully pull cardboard out and tie a 15-inch- (38-cm-) long piece of yarn firmly around the middle of the bundle to secure.

Cut the loops along the opposite untied edge. Fluff yarn.

Trim pompom, making sure not to cut the tie you used to secure the middle.

Attach the pompom to the hat, using the yarn tie to secure in place.

FINISHED MEASUREMENTS

10 × 11 inches (25 × 28 cm)

LEVEL OF EXPERIENCE

Absolute Beginner (time
    to complete: 30 to 60
    minutes)

MATERIALS

Big Loop Mini by Loopy
    Mango, 10 ounce
    (280 g) balls each
    30 yards (27 m)

1 ball in Heather Grey

US size 36 (20 mm) circular
    needles, 24 inches
    (60 cm) long

Tip: As with most projects,
    if you have a needle size
    that is close, such as
    US 35 (19 mm) for this
    project, the 1 mm will
    not make too much of
    a difference with such
    chunky yarns, so there's
    no need to buy the exact
    size needles.

GAUGE

2 sts = 2 inches (5 cm)
2 rows = 2 inches (5 cm)

The Helsinki Hat is one of the easiest and fastest projects in this book. If you know how to knit, you can easily make this lovely hat in less than an hour. And even if you don't, you can still make it with just a little more time. This pattern requires only one stitch: the knit stitch. It's so fast to make—it went viral in Korea, and even celebrities and K-pop stars were wearing it! This hat got its name from the Winter Olympics that took place in Helsinki. This hat is also incredibly warm, as it is knit with our thick Big Loop yarn.

Cast on 16 sts.

Join yarn to work in the rnd, being careful not to twist sts. Place marker.

RND 1 TO 11: K16.

RND 12: K2tog until the end (total 8 sts).

RND 13: K8 sts.

Finishing

Cut the yarn, leaving about 4 to 5 inches (10 to 13 cm). Pull the end through every st on the needle, remove the needle, then pull on the end to tighten up the top of the hat. Secure and fasten off.

HELSINKI
HAT

DOG
LEASH

MATERIALS

Big Loop Mini by Loopy Mango, 10 ounce (280 g) skeins each 30 yards (27 m)

S: 9½ yards (8.5 m) in Emerald

L: 14 yards (13 m) in Emerald

12 mm crochet hook

One brass O-ring (about 1 inch [2.5 cm])

S: One small brass snap hook 2 inch (5 cm)

L: One large brass snap hook 3 inch (7.5 cm)

Felting needle (optional)

I designed this dog leash for my beloved German shepherd named Loopy. She is no longer with us but will forever be in my heart. Loopy was a girl but everyone thought she was a boy, so I wanted to make a leash that would make her look more feminine while we were out walking. It's such a fun and easy project that we just had to include it—even though it's not a knitting piece! This is the only crocheted project in the book, and you don't even need to know how to crochet to make it. It comes in two sizes—small for small- or medium-size dogs and large for medium- and large-size dogs. The difference is that for the bigger dogs, the leash is thicker and shorter to give you more control. Big Loop is a great choice for this project, because it is much stronger than it looks. It's not just wool; it also has a strong cotton core inside. To make the fibers extra strong, you can put it in the washer and dryer when you are finished to felt it. And if it gets dirty, just throw it in the washer and dryer again! I have a German shepherd named Wolfie now, and he has these leashes in many different colors. He weighs 114 pounds, and they're strong enough even for him.

SIZE S

Make the Handle

Leaving a 10-inch (25-cm) tail, make a slip knot on the crochet hook. Ch15, then sl st into first chain to form a circle.

Make the Leash

Take the crochet hook out of the st loop and place the O-ring over the loop. Reinsert the crochet hook in the loop and ch40. Take the crochet hook out and place the ring end of the small snap hook over the loop. Reinsert the crochet hook in the loop and attach the snap hook to the leash as follows: Ch1, skip first ch, sl st into next 5 ch going backward toward the handle. Leaving a 10-inch (25-cm) tail, cut the yarn; fasten off.

SIZE L

Make the Leash

Leaving a 10-inch (25-cm) tail, make a slip knot on the crochet hook; ch30.

Starting with the tail, thread the ring end of the large snap hook through the ch and push the snap hook all the way up to the crochet hook. Attach the snap hook to the leash as follows: Ch1, skip first ch, then reinsert hook into next ch and work sl st in next 29 ch to the end.

Make the Handle

Take the crochet hook out of the st loop and place the O-ring over the loop. Reinsert the crochet hook in the loop. Ch15, then sl st into first ch of leash to attach the ch and form a circle.

Ch1, turn the work, skip 1 ch, sl st into next 15 ch going back around handle to make a 2nd row of sts. Leaving a 10 inch (25 cm) tail, cut the yarn; fasten off.

Finishing (Both Sizes)

Wrap both tail ends around the leash below the handle and below the snap hook. Tuck in the ends. If you have a felting needle, you can use it to felt in the ends of yarn for a cleaner look.

Wash the leash in a washing machine in hot water and tumble dry to felt it.

POMPOM
KEY CHAIN

4 inches (10 cm) in diameter
(pompom only)

LEVEL OF EXPERIENCE

Absolute Beginner (time to
complete: 30 minutes)

MATERIALS

Merino No. 5 by Loopy
Mango, 5.3 ounce
(150 g) balls each
74 yards (68 m)

1 ball (makes 6 pompoms) in
Mrs. Orange, Sunshine,
or Spicy Hot Pink

Snap hooks

Key rings (optional)

The Pompom Key Chain is the absolute fastest project in the book. There's not even any knitting! You only need scissors. It is a great accessory and very practical—a great way to help make sure you never lose your keys again. It could also be fun to add a few to your handbag or the Dog Leash (see page 48), as it doesn't have to be just one pompom. Make as many as you want to put on the same key chain or wherever else you'd like.

POMPOM (MAKES 1; SEE ALSO PAGE 172)

Cut a piece of cardboard to measure
4 × 6 inches (10 × 15 cm).

Using the short end of the cardboard,
wrap yarn around the cardboard
30 to 50 times.

Carefully pull cardboard out and tie
a 15-inch- (38-cm-) long piece of
yarn firmly around the middle of the
bundle to secure.

Cut the loops along the opposite
untied edge with scissors. Fluff yarn.

Trim pompom, making sure not to
cut the tie you used to secure the
middle.

Finishing

Use the tie end of the yarn to attach
the pompom to the ring end of
the snap hook. Slip the key ring
(optional) onto the other end of the
snap hook.

ABSOLUTE BEGINNER

BEGINNER

FINISHED

8 × 12 inches
(20 cm × 30.5 cm)

LEVEL OF EXPERIENCE

Beginner (time to complete:
1 to 2 hours)

MATERIALS

Merino No. 5 by Loopy
Mango, 5.3 ounce
(150 g) balls each 74
yard (68 m)

1 ball in Spicy Hot Pink

US 15 (10 mm) circular
needles, 16 inches
(40 cm) or 20 inches
(50 cm) long

GAUGE

10 sts = 5½ inches (14 cm)

10 rows = 3½ inches
(9 cm)

TIP

If you have any leftover yarn
(any yarn will work—even
a mix of different colors
or textures), make
a pompom. Tie your
pompom with a bow so
you can take it off and
you will have two styles
in one—some days wear
it with the pompom and
some days without.

The Her Beanie uses a rib stitch and is knit in the round. If you have not knit a rib stitch before, we recommend that you practice the knit stitch, practice the purl stitch, then practice combining knit and purl. When you feel confident about making the rib pattern, unravel your practice stitches and cast on for the beanie. There are many ways you can style it—you can wear it slouchy, fold it, etc. This style is unisex and is easily a must-have item for fall and winter. Both the stitch and the style are classic, but what makes this design special is the thick yarn it's made with.

Cast on 36 sts. Join yarn to work in the rnd, being careful not to twist sts. Place marker.

RND 1 TO 29: *K1, P1; rep from * to end.

RND 30: *K3tog, P1; rep from * to end (total 18 sts).

RND 31: *K1, P1; rep from * to end.

Finishing

Cut the yarn, leaving about 10 inches (25 cm). Pull the end through every st on the needle, remove the needle, then pull on the end to tighten up the top of the hat. Secure and fasten off.

HER
BEANIE

TWO-TONE POMPOM BEANIE

7½ × 10 inches
(19 × 25 cm)

LEVEL OF EXPERIENCE

Beginner (time to complete:
1 to 2 hours)

MATERIALS

Merino No. 5 by Loopy
Mango, 5.3 ounce
(150 g) balls each
74 yards (68 m)

2 balls, one in Polar Bear,
one in Mrs. Orange (you
can make up to two hats
with 2 balls of yarn; you
need 2 colors for color
blocking)

US 15 (10 mm) circular
needles, 16 inches
(40 cm) or 20 inches
(50 cm) long

GAUGE

10 sts = 5½ inches (14 cm)

10 rows = 3½ inches
(9 cm)

Color blocking always does magic and is so much fun! This pattern is very similar to Her Beanie, but by doing half of the beanie in one color and half in another and adding a pompom, it looks completely different. Don't be afraid to experiment with colors.

Col A: bottom of hat

Col B: top of hat

With Col A, cast on 34 sts. Join yarn to work in the rnd, being careful not to twist sts. Place marker.

RND 1 TO 15: *K1, P1; rep from * to end.

With Col B:

RND 16-28: *K1, P1; rep from * to end.

RND 29: *K2tog; rep from * to end (total 17 sts).

Finishing

Cut the yarn, leaving about 4 to 5 inches (10 to 13 cm). Pull the end through every st on the needle, remove the needle, then pull on the end to tighten up the top of the hat. Secure and fasten off.

POMPOM (SEE ALSO PAGE 172)

Cut a piece of cardboard 3 × 5 inches (7.5 × 13 cm).

Wrap remaining yarn around the short end of the cardboard.

Carefully pull cardboard out and tie yarn in the middle with a piece of yarn about 12 inches (30.5 cm) long.

Cut the loops along the opposite untied edge with scissors. Fluff yarn.

Trim pompom, making sure not to cut the tie you used to secure the middle.

Tie pompom to hat.

FINISHED MEASUREMENTS

19 × 5 inches (48 × 13 cm),
    does not include ties

LEVEL OF EXPEREINCE

Beginner (time to complete:
    1 to 2 hours)

MATERIALS

Mohair So Soft by Loopy
    Mango, 1.8 ounce
    (50 g) balls each
    65 yards (60 m)

1 ball in My Valentine

US size 15 (10 mm) straight
    or circular needles, any
    length

GAUGE

5 sts = 2 inches (5 cm)

6 rows = 2 inches (5 cm)

We love to wear hats, but maybe you are not a hat person or just want something different. This mohair headband is a great alternative that can be styled any way you wish. I have always admired the effortless, chic style of French women. Just a simple accessory such as a scarf or a headband can make a difference in your outfit. We all need some playfulness without spending too much time to make it. This headband is just it!

Tie

Cast on 3 sts.

ROW 1: K3.

ROW 2: P3.

Rep ROW 1 AND 2 until Tie measures
    10 inches (25 cm) long.

Do not bind off; keep knitting.

Band

ROW 1: KFB, K1, KFB.

ROW 2: P5.

ROW 3: KFB, K3, KFB.

ROW 4: P7.

ROW 5: KFB, K5, KFB.

ROW 6: P9.

ROW 7: KFB, K7, KFB.

ROW 8: P11.

ROW 9: KFB, K9, KFB.

ROW 10: P13.

ROW 11: K13.

ROW 12: P13.

ROW 13 TO 44: Rep ROW 11 AND 12.

ROW 45: K2TOG, K9, K2TOG.

ROW 46: P11.

ROW 47: K2TOG, K7, K2TOG.

ROW 48: P9.

ROW 49: K2TOG, K5, K2TOG.

ROW 50: P7.

ROW 51: K2TOG, K3, K2TOG.

ROW 52: P5.

ROW 53: K2TOG, K1, K2TOG.

Do not bind off; keep knitting.

Tie

ROW 54: K3.

ROW 55: P3.

Rep ROW 54 AND 55 until Tie
    measures 10 inches (25 cm) long.

Bind off.

Finishing

See finishing instructions on
    page 173.

MOHAIR
HEADBAND

WINTER SCARF

17 × 80 inches
(43 × 200 cm)

LEVEL OF EXPERIENCE

Beginner (time to complete:
3 to 5 hours)

MATERIALS

Merino No. 5 by Loopy
Mango, 5.3 ounce
(150 g) balls each
74 yards (68 m)

3 balls in Dorian Gray

US size 50 (25 mm) circular
needles, at least 24
inches (60 cm) long,
or US size 50 (25 mm)
straight needles, at
least 11 inches (28 cm)
long

GAUGE

1 st = 1 inch (2.5 cm)

4 rows = 3 inches (7.5 cm)

The soft and luxurious look of this oversize scarf is achieved by knitting the piece on a much larger needle size than normal. The majority of our projects stitched with Merino No. 5 yarn use US size 19 (15 mm) needles, but if you go up to US size 50 (25 mm) needles you will see a dramatic difference—a very soft, bouncy, and squishy knit that drapes beautifully and comes out larger in size.

Cast on 20 sts.

ROW 1 TO 4: K20 (makes 2 garter st ridges).

ROW 5: P20.

ROW 6: K20.

Rep ROW 5 AND 6 (working in St st) until you have 14 yards (13 m) of yarn left.

NEXT 4 ROWS: K20 (makes 2 garter st ridges).

Bind off.

Finishing

See finishing instructions on page 173.

30 × 70 inches
    (76 × 178 cm)

LEVEL OF EXPERIENCE

Beginner (time to complete:
    6 to 10 hours)

MATERIALS

Mohair So Soft by Loopy
    Mango, 1.8 ounce
    (50 g) balls each
    65 yards (60 m)

8 balls in Moss

US size 19 (15 mm) circular
    needles, at least
    20 inches (50 cm) long

GAUGE

5 sts = 3 inches (7.5 cm)

5 rows = 2 inches (5 cm)

The special beauty of mohair comes from its warmth, its lightness, and the brilliant colors you can dye this fiber. No other fiber takes the dye so well and in the same way. This mohair wrap is a staple for any wardrobe—it is very warm, yet light as a feather.

Cast on 50 sts.

ROW 1 TO 20: *K1, P1; rep from * to
    end.

ROW 21: K50.

ROW 22: P50.

ROW 23 TO 128: Rep ROW 21 AND
    22.

ROW 129 TO 148: Rep ROW 1.

Bind off.

Finishing

See finishing instructions on
    page 173.

HER
FRINGE
SHAWL

FINISHED MEASUREMENTS

62 × 28 inches
(157.5 × 71 cm)
(without the fringe)

LEVEL OF EXPERIENCE

Beginner (time to complete:
3 to 5 hours)

MATERIALS

Merino No. 5 by Loopy
Mango, 5.3 ounce
(150 g) balls each
74 yards (68 m)

4 balls in Midnight

US size 36 (20 mm)
needles *or* US size
35 (19 mm) circular
needles, 24 inches
(60 cm) long

GAUGE

3 sts = 2 inches (5 cm)

6 rows = 3 inches (7.5 cm)

TIP

Use a stitch marker to mark
the side where you are
working the decreases
and increases; this way
you don't have to keep it
in your head.

Scarves are great, but a shawl can give you many more options when it comes to styling. This shawl is worked in garter stitch and is enhanced with a fringe, making it more playful and fun. You'll start knitting from one of the corners, then just increase every other row until you reach the middle when you then start decreasing every other row to the end. Piece of cake!

Cast on 3 sts.

ROW 1: K3.

ROW 2: K3.

ROW 3 AND ALL ODD ROWS: KFB (increase), K to end.

ROW 4 AND ALL EVEN ROWS: K to end.

ROW 5–64: Rep ROW 3 AND 4.

ROW 65 AND 66: K all sts.

ROW 67 AND ALL ODD ROWS: K2TOG, K to end.

ROW 68 AND ALL EVEN ROWS: K to end.

ROW 69–128: Rep ROW 67 AND 68.

ROW 129 AND 130: K3.

Bind off.

Finishing

MAKE FRINGE

Cut remaining yarn into 70 pieces, each 22 inches (56 cm) long. Fold each piece in half to make a loop. Attach to shawl by pushing the loop ends through the outside edges of shawl and bringing the free ends back though the loop. Tighten fringe by pulling on the ends. Evenly space the fringe around the two shorter edges of the shawl. (See page 171.)

19 × 12 inches
(48 × 30.5 cm)

LEVEL OF EXPERIENCE

Beginner (time to complete:
1 to 2 hours)

MATERIALS

Merino No. 5 by Loopy
Mango, 5.3 ounce
(150 g) balls each
74 yards (68 m)

1 ball in Sunshine

US size 19 (15 mm) circular
needles, at least
20 inches (50 cm) long

2 wood or other decorative
beads with large
opening

GAUGE

3 sts = 2 inches (5 cm)

6 rows = 3 inches (7.5 cm)

Willie Nelson was my inspiration. I am a big fan of his music and he always wears a bandana, so I wanted to make my own version of a knitted bandana.

Cast on 3 sts.

ROW 1: K3.

ROW 2: P3.

ROW 3: *K1, M1; rep from * once
more, K1.

ROW 4: P5.

ROW 5: K1, M1, knit until 1 st
remains, M1, K1.

ROW 6: P7.

ROW 7: K3, M1, K1, M1, K3.

ROW 8: P9.

ROW 9: K4, M1, K1, M1, K4.

ROW 10: P11.

ROW 11: K5, M1, K1, M1, K5.

ROW 12: P13.

ROW 13: K6, M1, K1, M1, K6.

ROW 14: P15.

ROW 15: K7, M1, K1, M1, K7.

ROW 16: P17.

ROW 17: K8, M1, K1, M1, K8.

ROW 18: P19.

ROW 19: K9, M1, K1, M1, K9.

ROW 20: P21.

ROW 21: K10, M1, K1, M1, K10.

ROW 22: P23.

ROW 23: K11, M1, K1, M1, K11.

ROW 24: P25.

ROW 25: K12, M1, K1, M1, K12.

ROW 26: P27.

ROW 27: K13, M1, K1, M1, K13.

Bind off.

Finishing

MAKE TIES
Using a crochet hook of any size,
work two long chains, each
18 inches (46 cm) long (see
page 174). Attach each chain to
pointed ends of the bandana. If
desired, slip a bead on each end
and knot end of chain to secure.

MAKE FRINGE
Cut remaining yarn into pieces
28 inches (71 cm) long. Fold
each piece in half to make a loop.
Attach to scarf by pushing the
loop ends through the outside
edges of scarf and bringing the
free ends back though the loop.
Tighten fringe by pulling on the
ends. Evenly space the fringe
around the two shorter edges of
the bandana. (See page 171.)

LITTLE
TRIANGLE
FRINGE
BANDANA

FISHERMAN RIB COWL

8½ × 13 inches
(21.5 × 33 cm)

LEVEL OF EXPERIENCE

Beginner (time to complete:
1 to 2 hours)

MATERIALS

Merino No. 5 by Loopy
Mango, 5.3 ounce
(150 g) balls each
74 yards (68 m)

1 ball in Red Riding Hood

US size 19 (15 mm) circular
needles, 16 inches
(40 cm) or 20 inches
(50 cm) long

GAUGE

4 sts = 4 inches (10 cm)

8 rows = 4 inches (10 cm)

FISHERMAN RIB STITCH

See pages 160–161
for K1B and P1B
instructions.

TIPS

A stitch marker is essential
when knitting this style.
If you don't have a stitch
marker, just use a piece
of yarn or thread in a
different color.

Making this cowl in the fisherman rib stitch will give you a chunkier and more three-dimensional look and feel compared to a traditional rib. It is achieved by alternating rows of regular knit and purl with rows of P1B and K1B—so simply insert the needle as if for a knit stitch but below the strand of yarn, and do the same for P1B on alternate rows.

Cast on 28 sts.

Join yarn to work in the rnd, being careful not to twist sts. Place marker.

RND 1: K28.

RND 2: *P1, K1B; rep from * to end.

RND 3: *P1B, K1, rep from * to end.

RND 4 TO 30: Rep RND 2 AND 3.

Bind off.

Finishing

See finishing instructions on page 173.

One size

25 inches (63 cm) ×
    25 inches (63 cm)

LEVEL OF EXPERIENCE

Beginner (time to complete:
    6 to 8 hours)

MATERIALS

Big Loop by Loopy Mango,
    40 ounce (1,110 g) balls
    each 125 yards (115 m)

2 balls in Heather Grey

US size 50 (25 mm) circular
    needles, 32 inches
    (80 cm) long

US size 50 (25 mm) circular
    needles, 24 inches
    (60 cm) long

GAUGE

3 sts = 4 inches (10 cm) in
    garter stitch

5 rows = 4 inches (10 cm)
    in garter stitch

TIP

We recommend knitting
    tighter for this project—
    this way the jacket won't
    stretch out as much
    when being worn.

The Little Monster's Jacket was the first jacket I designed, and it is the easiest jacket to make in this book. I wanted a design that even a beginner knitter could easily make. It is worked in knit stitches only; the back is a simple rectangle, and the front panels are also rectangles. The name Little Monster comes from Lady Gaga fans. This jacket is for someone who wants to be different and unique—just like Gaga and her fans.

Back

Cast on 18 sts using longer
    (32 inch [82 cm]) knitting needles.

ROW 1 TO 37: K18.

Do NOT bind off.

Right Front

SHAPE NECK
Continue working on the first 9 sts
    only:

ROW 38: K9; turn the work, leaving
    remaining 9 sts on longer needles.

ROW 39 TO 74: K9, using shorter
    24 inch (60 cm) knitting needles

Bind off.

Left Front

SHAPE NECK
Reattach remaining yarn, and work
    on second set of 9 sts.

ROW 38 TO 74: K9.

Bind off.

CONTINUES

LITTLE
MONSTER'S
JACKET

Sleeves

Join FRONT and BACK together at side seams. To find shoulder line, fold the sweater in half, placing FRONT on top of BACK, and place markers on outside edges of shoulder line. Count down 14 rows from shoulder marker on each side for armhole openings, and place markers. Join side seams together below markers, leaving an opening 5 inches (13 cm) up from the bottom for side slits on each side.

With shorter circular needles, pick up 14 sts (1 st every other row) evenly spaced around each armhole (7 sts each on FRONT and BACK) starting at underarm area and working counterclockwise.

Join yarn to work in the rnd. Place marker.

RND 1 TO 8: K14.

Bind off.

Finishing

See finishing instructions on page 173.

NANTUCKET THROW

36 × 70 inches
(91 × 178 cm)

LEVEL OF EXPERIENCE

Beginner (time to complete:
4 to 6 hours)

MATERIALS

Big Loop by Loopy Mango,
40 ounce (1,100 g)
balls each 125 yards
(115 m)

2 balls in Ivory (or 1 ball for
smaller-size blanket)

US size 50 (25 mm)
needles, at least 32 in
(80 cm) long, either
circular or straight

GAUGE

10 sts = 15 inches (38 cm)

1 rows = 1 inch (2.5 cm)

TIP

For best results, knit
loosely.

The Nantucket Throw was the first blanket pattern I designed, and it became an instant trend in the knitting world and was incredibly popular in interior design. It seemed people were drawn largely to its scale and beauty. I wanted to keep it super simple so that it was very easy for any beginner knitter to accomplish, yet still a beautiful design. You can even make a smaller lap blanket size (approximately 28 × 40 inches [71 × 101.5 cm]) using just one skein of Big Loop yarn instead. Just follow this same pattern but cast on 18 stitches instead of 26. It is very important to knit loosely for this project and to bind off loosely, as well.

Cast on 26 sts.

ROW 1: K2, *P2, K2; rep from * to
end.

ROW 2: P2, *K2, P2; rep from * to
end.

Rep ROW 1 AND 2 until you have
4 yards (4 m) of yarn left.

Bind off very loosely in rib pattern.

Finishing

See finishing instructions on
page 173.

44 × 68 inches
(112 × 172.5 cm)

LEVEL OF EXPERIENCE

Beginner (time to complete:
7 to 14 hours)

MATERIALS

Merino No. 5 by Loopy
Mango, 5.3 ounce
(150 g) balls each
74 yards (68 m)

8 balls in Iceberg

US size 50 (25 mm) circular
needles, at least
32 inches (81 cm) long

GAUGE

6 sts = 7 inches (18 cm)

6 rows = 3 inches (7.5 cm)

I love knitting throws and blankets, and I wanted a blanket that was very squishy and three-dimensional. Fisherman rib stitch is perfect for this—it is so much thicker than regular rib. It does use more yarn than regular rib, but the end result is totally worth it!

Cast on 40 sts.

ROW 1: P40.

ROW 2: *P1, K1B; rep from * to end of row.

Rep ROW 2 until throw reaches 67 inches (170 cm) long, leaving about 6 yards (5.5) m to bind off.

Bind off.

Finishing

See finishing instructions on
page 173.

FISHERMAN
RIB THROW

INTERMEDIATE

12 × 90 inches
(30.5 × 228.5 cm)

LEVEL OF EXPERIENCE

Intermediate (time to
complete: 4 to 5 hours)

MATERIALS

Merino No. 5 by Loopy
Mango, 5.3 ounce
(150 g) balls each
74 yards (68 m)

Color A: 2 balls in Midnight
Blue; Color B: 2 balls in
Polar Bear

US size 50 (25 mm) circular
needles, at least
24 inches (60 cm) long
or straight needles
11 inches (28 cm) long

GAUGE

Flower = 3 inches (7.5 cm)
in diameter

Flower with border =
4½ inches (11.5 cm)
in diameter

ASTER FLOWER MOTIF

See pages 166–167 for
an illustration of Row 2
and 3.

Slip next 5 stitches to right
needle, dropping extra
loops.

Slip these 5 stitches back
to left needle.

P1, yo, P1, yo, P1. Work all
5 stitches together without
removing them from the
needle (you will end with
5 stitches on the right
needle).

It's easy to assume that this pattern is crocheted rather than knitted. But it is actually all stitched with knitting needles. This beautiful stitch is called the Aster Flower. Once you have mastered making knit and purl stitches, you are officially ready to try your hand at the Aster Flower—just be patient with it, and the results will most definitely be worth it.

Col A: Border Color

Col B: Flower Color

With Color A, cast on 19 sts.

ROW 1: (Wrong Side) With Color A, K19.

ROW 2: (Right Side) With Col B, SL 1, * K5 (wrapping yarn twice around needle for each st), SL 1; rep from * two more times.

ROW 3: With Col B, SL 1, *work one Aster Flower Motif, SL 1; rep from * two more times.

ROW 4: With Col A, K1, *K5, knit the next stitch with the loose strand in back; rep from * one more time, K6.

ROW 5: With Col A, K19.

ROW 6: With Col B, SL 4, *K5 (wrapping yarn twice around needle for each st), SL 1, rep from * once more, SL 3.

ROW 7: With Col B, SL 4, *work one Aster Flower Motif, SL 1; rep from * once more, SL 3.

ROW 8: With Col A, K9, knit next stitch with the loose strand in back, K9.

ROW 9: With Col A, K19.

Rep ROW 2 TO 9 until you have at least 5 yards/4.5 m of each color left.

Rep ROW 2 TO 4.

Bind off.

Finishing

See finishing instructions on page 173.

ASTER
FLOWER
SCARF

ASTER
FLOWER
BLANKET

40 × 65 inches
(101.5 × 165 cm)

LEVEL OF EXPERIENCE

Intermediate (time to
complete: 8 to 12
hours)

MATERIALS

Merino No. 5 by Loopy
Mango, 5.3 ounce
(150 g) balls each
74 yards (68 m)

Col A: 4 balls in Café con
Leche; Col B: 5 balls in
Jungle

US size 50 (25 mm)
needles, at least
32 inches (80 cm) long

GAUGE

Flower = 3 inches (7.5 cm)
in diameter

Flower with border =
4½ inches (11.5 cm)
in diameter

ASTER FLOWER MOTIF

See pages 166–167 for
an illustration of Row 2
and 3.

Slip next 5 stitches to right
needle, dropping extra
loops.

Slip these 5 stitches back
to left needle.

P1, yo, P1, yo, P1. Work all
5 stitches together without
removing them from the
needle (you will end with
5 stitches on the right
needle).

This beautiful stitch is stitched with knitting needles, despite looking like a crochet pattern. The pattern is great for any size blanket or throw and will make a statement in your home. Use two neutral colors together for a subtler effect or a neutral border with a bright flower color to make it pop.

Col A: Border Color

Col B: Flower Color

With Col A, cast on 61 sts.

ROW 1: (Wrong Side) With Col A,
K61.

ROW 2: (Right Side) With Col B,
SL 1, *K5 (wrapping yarn twice
around needle for each st), SL 1;
rep from * to end.

ROW 3: With Col B, SL 1, *work one
Aster Flower Motif, SL 1; rep from
* to end.

ROW 4: With Col A, K1, *K5, knit the
next st with the loose strand in
back; rep from * to last 6 sts, K6.

ROW 5: With Col A, K61.

ROW 6: With Col B, SL 4, *K5
(wrapping yarn twice around
needle for each st), SL 1; rep from
* to last 3 sts, SL 3.

ROW 7: With Col B, SL 4, *work one
Aster Flower Motif, SL 1; rep from
* to last 3 sts, SL 3.

ROW 8: With Col A, K4, *K5, knit next
st with the loose strand in back;
rep from * to last 9 sts, K9.

ROW 9: With Col A, K61.

ROW 10 TO 81: Rep ROW 2 TO 9.

ROW 82 TO 88: Rep ROW 2 TO 8.

Bind off.

Finishing

See finishing instructions on page
173.

One size

Chest (side seam to side
  seam): 24 inches
  (61 cm)

Length: 22 inches (56 cm)

LEVEL OF EXPERIENCE

Intermediate (time to
  complete: 8 to 12
  hours)

MATERIALS

Merino No. 5 by Loopy
  Mango, 5.3 ounce
  (150 g) balls each
  74 yards (68 m)

7 balls in Cafe con Leche

US size 19 (15 mm) circular
  needles, at least 24
  inches (60 cm) long

GAUGE

4 sts = 3 inches (7.5 cm)

4 rows = 2 inches (5 cm)

When I think about a cozy winter sweater, this oversized style immediately comes to mind. It is soft, warm, and easy to coordinate with any outfit—it works well with pants, a dress, or a skirt. This is guaranteed to become a winter wardrobe staple. It's also one of our easiest sweaters—the back and front are essentially two rectangles joined together on the sides, and the sleeves are made by picking up stitches around the armhole and knitting in the round (just like making a beanie!).

Tip: If you aren't a fan of turtlenecks, simply knit fewer rows for the neck and you will end up with a mock-neck sweater instead. The number of fewer rows knitted is completely up to you.

Back

Cast on 35 sts.

ROW 1: K1, *P1, K1; rep from * to
  end.

ROW 2: P1, *K1, P1; rep from * to
  end.

ROWS 3–6: Rep ROW 1 AND 2.

ROW 7: K35.

ROW 8: P35.

ROW 9 TO 46: Rep ROW 7 AND 8
  (working in St st).

ROW 47: K35.

Bind off.

Front

Cast on 35 sts.

ROW 1: K1, *P1, K1; rep from * to
  end.

ROW 2: P1, *K1, P1; rep from * to
  end.

ROWS 3–6: Rep ROW 1 AND 2.

ROW 7: K35.

ROW 8: P35.

ROW 9 TO 42: Rep ROW 7 AND 8
  (working in St st).

CONTINUES

SHAPE RIGHT NECK

ROW 43: K14; turn the work, leaving remaining 21 sts on the needle or on a piece of waste yarn.

ROW 44: P14.

ROW 45: K12, K2TOG.

ROW 46: P13.

ROW 47: K11, K2TOG.

Bind off.

SHAPE LEFT NECK

Reattach yarn. Bind off 7 sts from the center, then continue to work on remaining 14 sts.

ROW 43: K14.

ROW 44: P14.

ROW 45: K2TOG, K12.

ROW 46: P13.

ROW 47: K2TOG, K11.

Bind off.

Sleeves

Join FRONT and BACK together at side seams. Count down 24 rows from shoulder marker on each side for armhole openings, and place markers. Join side seams together below markers.

With circular needles, pick up 24 sts (1 st every other row) evenly spaced around each armhole (12 sts each on FRONT and BACK) starting at underarm area and working clockwise. Join yarn to work in the rnd. Place marker.

RND 1 TO 35: K24.

RND 36: *K2TOG, P2TOG; rep from * to end (total 12 sts).

RND 37 TO 39: *K1, P1; rep from * to end of rnd.

Bind off.

Finishing

TURTLENECK

With circular needles, pick up 26 sts evenly around neckline, working clockwise. Join yarn to work in the rnd. Place marker.

RND 1 TO 12: *K1, P1; rep from * to end.

Bind off loosely in rib pattern.

See additional finishing instructions on page 173.

ON POINT TUNIC

One size

Chest (side seam to side seam): 23½ inches (59.5 cm)

Length: 25 inches (63.5 cm)

Intermediate (time to complete: 11 to 15 hours)

Merino No. 5 by Loopy Mango, 5.3 ounce (150 g) balls each 74 yards (68 m)

Main Col: 8 balls in Polar Bear, Accent Col: 1 ball in Spicy Hot Pink

US size 19 (15 mm) needles, at least 24 inches (60 cm) long

6 sts = 4 inches (10 cm)

11 rows = 4 inches (10 cm)

I love to experiment with color blocking. Just a few rows of a contrasting color can give a design a completely different character. I like the pop of an accent color, so I usually choose hot pink, neon yellow, bright red, or orange. You can also choose more of a neutral shade such as a gray or beige to tone it down. I wanted to design something basic but edgy at the same time— something you can throw over a pair of jeans and look effortlessly chic in. With this piece, you can be fashionably on point without trying too hard.

Back

With Main Col, cast on 35 sts.

ROW 1: K1, *P1, K1; rep from * to end.

ROW 2: P1, *K1, P1; rep from * to end.

ROW 3 TO 10: Rep ROWS 1 AND 2.

ROW 11 TO 76: K35.

Bind off.

Front

With Main Col, cast on 35 sts.

ROW 1: K1, *P1, K1; rep from * to end.

ROW 2: P1, *K1, P1; rep from * to end.

ROW 3 TO 10: Rep ROW 1 AND 2.

ROW 11 TO 48: K35.

Change to Accent Col.

ROW 49 TO 60: K35.

Change to Main Col.

ROW 61 TO 70: K35.

SHAPE RIGHT FRONT NECK

ROW 71: K11; turn work, leaving remaining 24 sts on a needle or on a piece of waste yarn.

ROW 72: K11.

ROW 73: K9, K2TOG.

ROW 74: K10.

ROW 75: K8, K2TOG.

ROW 76: K9.

Bind off.

SHAPE LEFT FRONT NECK

Reattach yarn. Bind off 13 sts in the center for back neck.

ROW 71: K11.

ROW 72: K11.

ROW 73: K2TOG, K9.

ROW 74: K10.

ROW 75: K2TOG, K8.

ROW 76: K9.

Bind off.

CONTINUES

Sleeves

Join FRONT and BACK together at shoulder and side seams. Count down 32 rows from shoulder on each side for armhole openings, and place markers. Join side seams together below markers.

With circular needles and Main Col, pick up 32 sts (1 st every other row) evenly around each armhole (16 sts each on FRONT and BACK) starting at underarm area and working clockwise. Join yarn to work in the rnd. Place marker.

RND 1: K32.

RND 2: P32.

RND 3 TO 36: Rep RND 1 AND 2.

RND 37: *K2TOG, P2TOG; rep from * to end.

RND 38 TO 39: *K1, P1; rep from * to end.

Bind off loosely in rib pattern.

Finishing

NECKBAND

With circular needles and Main Col, pick up 38 sts evenly around the neckline, working clockwise. Join yarn to work Neckband in the rnd. Place marker.

RND 1 TO 15: *K1, P1; rep from * to end.

Bind off loosely in rib pattern.

See additional finishing instructions on page 173.

One size

Chest (side seam to side
    seam): 23 inches
    (58 cm)

Length: 20 inches (51 cm)

LEVEL OF EXPERIENCE

Intermediate (time to
    complete: 8 to 16
    hours)

MATERIALS

Merino No. 5 by Loopy
    Mango, 5.3 ounce
    (150 g) balls each
    74 yards (68 m)

6 balls in Bordeaux

US size 19 (15 mm) circular
    needles at least
    24 inches (60 cm) long

GAUGE

4 sts = 3 inches (7.5 cm)

4 rows = 2 inches (5 cm)

I have a pair of cowboy boots, and I wanted to design something I could wear with them—something not too long, not too short, and with a fringe just like in a cowboy jacket. This is my interpretation of urban cowboy style.

Back

Cast on 35 sts.

ROW 1: K1, *P1, K1; rep from * to end.

ROW 2: P1, *K1, P1; rep from * to end.

ROW 3 TO 10: Rep ROW 1 AND 2.

ROW 11: K35.

ROW 12: P35.

ROW 13 TO 16: Rep ROW 11 AND 12.

ROW 17 TO 20: K35.

ROW 21 TO 24: Rep ROW 11 AND 12.

ROW 25 TO 28: K35.

ROW 29 TO 32: Rep ROW 11 AND 12.

ROW 33: K2TOG, K31, K2TOG.

ROW 34: K33.

ROW 35: K2TOG, K29, K2TOG.

ROW 36: K31.

ROW 37: K2TOG, K27, K2TOG.

ROW 38: P29.

ROW 39: K29.

ROW 40 TO 41: Rep ROW 38 AND 39.

ROW 42: P29.

ROW 43 TO 54: K29.

Bind off.

Front

Cast on 35 sts.

Work same as BACK up to ROW 48.

SHAPE RIGHT NECK

ROW 49 TO 50: K10; turn work, leaving remaining 25 sts on the needle or on a piece of waste yarn.

ROW 51: K8, K2TOG.

ROW 52: K9.

ROW 53: K7, K2TOG.

ROW 54: K8.

Bind off.

CONTINUES

URBAN
COWBOY
SWEATER

SHAPE LEFT NECK

Reattach yarn. Bind off 9 sts in the
center for back neck. (The last st
of your bind-off is the first st of
ROW 49.)

ROWS 49 TO 50: K10.

ROW 51: K2TOG, K8.

ROW 52: K9.

ROW 53: K2TOG, K7.

ROW 54: K8.

Bind off.

Sleeves

Join FRONT and BACK together
at shoulder seams and side
seams. Count down 28 rows from
shoulder on each side for armhole
openings, and place marker.
Join side seams together below
markers.

With circular needles, pick up
28 sts (1 st every other row)
evenly spaced around each
armhole (14 sts each on FRONT
and BACK) starting at underarm
area and working clockwise. Join
yarn to work in the rnd. Place
marker.

RND 1: K28.

RND 2: P28.

RND 3 TO 20: Rep RND 1 AND 2.

RND 21 TO 26: K28.

RND 27: P28.

RND 28: K28.

RND 29 TO 36: Rep RND 27 AND 28.

RND 37 TO 38: K28.

RND 39: *K2TOG, P2TOG; rep from
* to end.

RND 40 TO 43: *K1, P1; rep from *
to end.

Bind off loosely in rib pattern.

Finishing

NECKBAND

Working clockwise, evenly pick up
36 sts around front and back neck
edges. Join yarn to work in the
rnd. Place marker.

RND 1 TO 3: *K1, P1; rep from * to
end.

Bind off in rib pattern.

See additional finishing instructions
on page 173.

MAKE FRINGE

Cut 26 pieces of yarn for FRONT
and 29 pieces for BACK, each
17 inches (43 cm) long. Fold
each piece in half to make a loop.
Attach to sweater by pushing the
loop ends through the sweater
from the front and bringing the
free ends back through the loop.
Tighten fringe by pulling on the
ends. (See page 171.)

Evenly space the fringe around the
sweater in 2 rows on FRONT and
BACK.

MERI-MOHAIR SWEATER

SIZE

S/M, M/L

FINISHED MEASUREMENTS

S/M

Chest (side seam to side seam): 21 inches (53 cm)

Length: 19 inches (48 cm)

M/L

Chest (side seam to side seam): 24 inches (61 cm)

Length: 23 inches (58 cm)

LEVEL OF EXPERIENCE

Intermediate (time to complete: 6 to 9 hours)

MATERIALS

Mohair So Soft by Loopy Mango, 1.8 ounce (50 g) balls each 65 yards (60 m)

2 (3) balls in Shameless Pink

Merino No. 5 by Loopy Mango, 5.3 ounce (150 g) balls each 74 yards (68 m)

3 (4) balls in Bubblegum

US size 19 (15 mm) circular needles, at least 20 inches (50 cm) long

GAUGE

Merino:

4 sts = 4 inches (10 cm)

6 rows = 3 inches (7.5 cm)

Mohair:

4 sts = 3 inches (7.5 cm)

8 rows = 3 inches (7.5 cm)

This is a great project to mix things up! By using different types of yarns in the same project, you can vary not only the colors but also the textures. Here we have stripes of merino wool alternating with stripes of mohair.

Front

With *Merino No. 5*, cast on 29(33) sts.

ROW 1: K1, *P1, K1; rep from * to end.

ROW 2: P1, *K1, P1; rep from * to end.

ROW 3 TO 4(8): Rep ROW 1 AND 2.

ROW 5(9): KFB, K27(31), KFB.

ROW 6(10): P31(35).

ROW 7(11): K31(35).

ROW 8(12): P31(35).

Change to *Mohair So Soft*.

ROW 9(13) TO 16(20): Rep ROW 7(11) AND 8(12).

Change to *Merino No. 5*.

ROW 17(21) TO 22(26): Rep ROW 7(11) AND 8(12).

Change to *Mohair So Soft*.

ROW 23(27) TO 30(34): Rep ROW 7(11) AND 8(12).

Change to *Merino No. 5*.

ROW 31(35): K31(35).

ROW 32(36): P31(35).

ROW 33(37): K2TOG, K27(31), K2TOG.

ROW 34(38): P29(33).

ROW 35(39): K2TOG, K25(29), K2TOG.

ROW 36(40): P27(31).

ROW 37(41): K27(31).

ROW 38(42): P27(31).

Change to *Mohair So Soft*.

ROW 39(43) TO 42(46): Rep ROW 37(41) AND 38(42).

Change to *Merino No. 5*.

ROW 43(47) TO 46(50): Rep ROW 37(41) AND 38(42).

Do not bind off.

CONTINUES

SHAPE RIGHT NECK

ROW 47(51): K8(10); turn, leaving remaining sts on needle or on a piece of waste yarn.

ROW 48(52): P8(10).

ROW 49(53): K6(8), K2TOG.

ROW 50(54): P7(9).

Bind off.

SHAPE LEFT NECK

With *Merino No. 5*, reattach yarn. Bind off 11 sts for center neck opening.

ROW 47(51): K8(10).

ROW 48(52): P8(10).

ROW 49(53): K2TOG, K6(8).

ROW 50(54): P7(9).

Bind off.

Back

With *Merino No. 5*, cast on 29(33) sts.

ROW 1: K1, *P1, K1; rep from * to end.

ROW 2: P1, *K1, P1; rep from * to end.

ROW 3 AND 4(8): Rep ROW 1 AND 2.

ROW 5(9): KFB, K27(31), KFB.

ROW 6(10): P31(35).

ROW 7(11): K31(35).

ROW 8(12): P31(35).

Change to *Mohair So Soft*.

ROW 9(13) TO 16(20): Rep ROW 7(11) AND 8(12).

Change to *Merino No. 5*.

ROW 17(21) TO 22(26): Rep ROW 7(11) AND 8(12).

Change to *Mohair So Soft*.

ROW 23(27) TO 30(34): Rep ROW 7(11) AND 8(12).

Change to *Merino No. 5*.

ROW 31(35): K31(35).

ROW 32(36): P31(35).

ROW 33(37): K2TOG, K27(31), K2TOG.

ROW 34(38): P29(33).

ROW 35(39): K2TOG, K25(29), K2TOG.

ROW 36(40): P27(31).

ROW 37(41): K27(31).

ROW 38(42): P27(31).

Change to *Mohair So Soft*.

ROW 39(43) TO 42(46): Rep ROW 37(41) AND 38(42).

Change to *Merino No. 5*.

ROW 43(47) TO 50(54): Rep ROW 37(41) AND 38(42).

Bind off.

Sleeves

Join FRONT and BACK together at shoulder and side seams. Count down 24 (26) rows from shoulder on each side for armhole openings, and place markers. Join side seams together below markers.

With circular needles and *Merino No. 5*, pick up 24(26) sts (1 st every other row) evenly spaced around each armhole (12[13] sts each on FRONT and BACK) starting at underarm area and working clockwise. Join yarn to work in the rnd, being careful not to twist sts. Place marker.

RND 1 TO 6: K24(26).

Change to *Mohair So Soft*.

RND 7 TO 12: K24(26).

Change to *Merino No. 5*.

RND 13 TO 18: K24(26).

Change to *Mohair So Soft*.

RND 19 TO 24: K24(26).

Change to *Merino No. 5*.

RND 25 TO 30: K24(26).

Change to *Mohair So Soft*.

RND 31 TO 36: K24(26).

Change to *Merino No. 5*.

RND 37 TO 38: K24(26).

RND 39: *K2TOG; rep from * to end.

RND 40: K12(13).

Bind off.

Finishing

NECKBAND

With circular needles and *Merino No. 5*, pick up 32(34) sts evenly around the neck edge, working clockwise to work in the rnd. Place marker.

RND 1 TO 3: *K1, P1; rep from * to end.

Bind off in rib pattern.

See additional finishing instructions on page 173.

MOHAIR LONG DRESS

One size

Chest (side seam to side seam): 27 inches (69 cm)

Length: 40 inches (101.5 cm)

LEVEL OF EXPERIENCE

Intermediate (time to complete: 11 to 16 hours)

MATERIALS

Mohair So Soft by Loopy Mango, 1.8 ounce (50 g) balls each 65 yards (60 m)

10 balls in Milk Tea

US size 19 (15 mm) circular needles, at least 24 inches (60 cm) long

US size K/10.5 (6.5 mm) crochet hook

GAUGE

5 sts = 3 inches (7.5 cm)

5 rows = 3 inches (7.5 cm)

Mohair is a very light and warm fiber. I wanted to make a simple and easy piece with it. This long dress is something I can just wear over a slip when I go out to walk the dog or run errands. It's great for lounging around the house, too.

Back

Cast on 49 sts.

ROW 1: K1, *P1, K1; rep from * to end.

ROW 2: P1, *K1, P1; rep from * to end.

ROW 3 AND 4: Rep ROW 1 AND 2.

ROW 5: K49.

ROW 6: P49.

ROW 7 TO 64: Rep ROW 5 AND 6 (working in St st).

ROW 65: K2TOG, K45, K2TOG.

ROW 66: P47.

ROW 67: K2TOG, K43, K2TOG.

ROW 68: P45.

ROW 69: K2TOG, K41, K2TOG.

ROW 70: P43.

ROW 71: K2TOG, K39, K2TOG.

ROW 72: P41.

ROW 73: K2TOG, K37, K2TOG.

ROW 74: P39.

ROW 75: K39.

ROW 76: P39.

ROW 77 TO 80: Rep ROW 75 AND 76.

Bind off.

CONTINUES

Front

Work same as for BACK.

Sleeves

Join FRONT and BACK together at shoulder and side seams. For shoulders measure 8 inches (20 cm) in from each side seam on FRONT and BACK, and place markers. Join the shoulders together along edges to marker, leaving about 10 inches (25 cm) for neck opening.

Count down 32 rows from shoulder on each side for armhole openings, and place markers. Join side seams together below markers.

With circular needles, pick up 32 sts (1 st every other row) evenly spaced around each armhole (16 sts each on FRONT and BACK) starting at underarm area and working clockwise. Join yarn to work in the rnd. Place marker.

RND 1 TO 35: K32.

RND 36: *K2TOG; rep from * to end.

RND 37: K16.

Bind off in rib pattern.

Finishing

With crochet hook, work a chain (see page 174) about 20 inches (51 cm) in length and attach one end to each side of neckline at point where shoulder seams join.

See additional finishing instructions on page 173.

FINISHED MEASUREMENTS

S/M

Chest (side seam to side seam): 21 inches (53 cm)

Front length (shoulder to hem): 19 inches (48 cm)

Back length (shoulder to hem): 18 inches (46 cm)

M/L

Chest (side seam to side seam): 24 inches (61 cm)

Front length (shoulder to hem): 22 inches (56 cm)

Back length (shoulder to hem): 21 inches (53 cm)

LEVEL OF EXPERIENCE

Intermediate (time to complete: 8 to 12 hours)

MATERIALS

Merino No. 5 by Loopy Mango, 5.3 ounce (150 g) balls each 74 yards (68 m)

6 balls in Butter for S/M; 7 balls in Butter for size M/L

US size 19 (15 mm) circular needles, at least 24 inches (60 cm) in length

US size 19 (15 mm) double pointed needle, to be used as cable needle

GAUGE

3 sts = 2 inches (5 cm)

5 rows = 2 inches (5 cm)

ABBREVIATIONS USED

T3F, T3B, C4F, C4B (see pages 162–163)

I love traditional fisherman sweaters, and this is my take on the style. I wanted to simplify it and make it more modern.

Note: for more on cables, see pages 162–163.

Front

Cast on 36(40) sts.

ROW 1: K3(5), P2, *K2, P2; rep from * until 3(5) sts remain, K3(5).

ROW 2: P3(5), K2, *P2, K2; rep from * until 3(5) sts remain, P3(5).

ROW 3 TO 12(16): Rep ROW 1 AND 2.

ROW 13(17): K6(8), P1, *T3F, T3B, P2; rep from * one more time, T3F, T3B, P1, K6(8).

ROW 14(18): K8(10), *P4, K4; rep from * one more time, P4, K8(10).

ROW 15(19): K6(8), P2, *C4F, P4; rep from * one more time, C4F, P2, K6(8).

ROW 16(20): Rep ROW 14(18).

ROW 17(21): K6(8), P1, *T3B, T3F, P2; rep from * one more time, T3B, T3F, P1, K6(8).

ROW 18(22): K7(9), *P2, K2; rep from * 4 more times, P2, K7(9).

ROW 19(23) TO 24 (28): Rep ROW 13(17) TO 18(22).

ROW 25(29): K6(8), *T3B, P2, T3F; rep from * two more times, K6(8).

ROW 26(30): K6(8), P2, *K4, P4; rep from * one more time, K4, P2, K6(8).

ROW 27(31): K8(10), *P4, C4B; rep from * one more time, P4, K8(10).

ROW 28(32): Rep ROW 26(30).

ROW 29(33): K8(10), P3, *T3B, T3F, P2; rep from * one more time, P1, K8(10).

ROW 30(34): K6(8), P2, K3, *P2, K2; rep from * 2 more times, P2, K3, P2, K6(8).

ROW 31(35): K8(10), P3, T3F, T3B, P2, T3F, T3B, P3, K8(10).

ROW 32(36): Rep ROW 26(30).

ROW 33(37): Rep ROW 27(31).

ROW 34(38): Rep ROW 26(30).

ROW 35(39): K6(8), *T3F, P2, T3B; rep from * 2 more times, K6(8).

ROW 36(40): Rep Row 18(22).

ROW 37(41): K6(8), P1, *T3F, T3B, P2; rep from * one more time, T3F, T3B, P1, K6(8).

ROW 38(42): K8(10), *P4, K4; rep from * one more time, P4, K8(10).

ROW 39(43): K6(8), P2, *C4F, P4; rep from * one more time, C4F, P2, K6(8).

ROW 40(44): Rep ROW 38(42).

ROW 41(45): K6(8), P1, *T3B, T3F, P2; rep from * one more time, T3B, T3F, P1, K6(8).

ROW 42(46): K7(9), *P2, K2; rep from * 4 more times, P2, K7(9).

ROW 43(47) TO 48(52): Rep ROWS 37(41) TO 42(46).

CONTINUES

URBAN
FISHERMAN
SWEATER

SHAPE RIGHT NECK

ROW 49(53): K6(8), T3B, P2, K2, P1; turn work, leaving remaining sts on the needle or on a piece of waste yarn.

ROW 50(54): K1, P2, K3, P2, K6(8).

ROW 51(55): K8(10), P3, K1, K2TOG.

ROW 52(56): P2, K3, P2, K6(8).

For S/M, bind off.

For M/L, continue:

ROW 57: K10, P3, K2TOG.

ROW 58: P1, K3, P2, K8.

Bind off.

SHAPE LEFT NECK

Reattach yarn. Bind off 8 sts in the center for neck. Purl the last st of bind off.

ROW 49(53): P1, K2, P2, T3F, K6(8).

ROW 50(54): K6(8), P2, K3, P3.

ROW 51(55): K2TOG, K1, P3, K8(10).

ROW 52(56): K6(8), P2, K3, P2.

For S/M, bind off.

For M/L, continue:

ROW 57: K2TOG, P3, K10.

ROW 58: K8, P2, K3, P1.

Bind off.

Back

Cast on 34(38) sts

ROW 1: K2(4), P2, *K2, P2; rep from * until 2(4) sts remain, K2(4).

ROW 2: P2(4), K2, *P2, K2; rep from * until 2(4) sts remain, P2(4).

ROW 3 TO 12(16): Rep ROWS 1 AND 2.

ROW 13(17) TO 52(58): K34(38).

Bind off.

CONTINUES

Sleeves

Join FRONT and BACK together at shoulder and side seams. Count down 24 rows from shoulder on each side for armhole openings, and place markers. Join side seams together below markers. Seam shoulders and sides.

With circular needles, pick up 24 sts (1 st every other row) evenly spaced around each armhole (12 sts each on FRONT and BACK) starting at underarm area and working clockwise. Join yarn to work in the rnd. Place marker.

RND 1: K24.

RND 2: P24.

RND 3 TO 36(42): Rep RND 1 AND 2.

RND 37(43): *K2TOG, P2TOG; rep from * to end.

RND 38(44) TO 42(48): *K1, P1; rep from * to end.

Bind off loosely in rib pattern.

Finishing

NECKBAND

With circular needles, pick up 28(30) sts evenly around neck opening, working clockwise, to knit in the rnd. Join yarn. Place marker.

RND 1 TO 5: *K1, P1; rep from * to end.

Bind off loosely in rib pattern.

See additional finishing instructions on page 173.

FINISHED MEASUREMENTS

S/M

Chest (side seam to side
    seam): 18 inches (46 cm)

Length: 16 inches (40.5 cm)

M/L

Chest (side seam to side
    seam): 22 inches (56 cm)

Length: 19 inches (48 cm)

LEVEL OF EXPERIENCE

Intermediate (time to
    complete: 4 to 8 hours)

MATERIALS

Merino No. 5 by Loopy
    Mango, 5.3 ounce
    (150 g) balls each
    74 yards (68 m)

4(5) balls in Red Riding
    Hood

US size 19 (15 mm) circular
    needles, at least
    32 inches (80 cm) long

GAUGE

10 sts = 7 inches (18 cm)

10 rows = 4 inches (10 cm)

This cardigan is adorable as well as very economical—it only uses four or five balls of yarn (depending on the size). A very versatile piece for any wardrobe, it looks equally great over a dress or a skirt, or with jeans and a turtleneck for a more casual look.

Back

Cast on 31(35) sts.

ROW 1: K1, *P1, K1; rep from * to end.

ROW 2: P1, *K1, P1; rep from * to end.

ROW 3 TO 10: Rep ROW 1 AND 2.

ROW 11 TO 40 (44): K1, *P1, K1; rep from * to end.

Do NOT bind off.

Right Front

SHAPE NECK

ROW 41(45): K1, *P1, K1; rep from * until you have worked 13(15) sts. Turn the work, leaving remaining 18(20) sts on the needle or on a piece of waste yarn.

ROW 42 TO 70 (46 TO 78): K1, *P1, K1; rep from * to end.

ROW 71 TO 79 (79 TO 87) ODD ROWS: K1, *P1, K1; rep from * to end.

ROW 72 TO 80 (80 TO 88) EVEN ROWS: P1, *K1, P1; rep from * to end.

Bind off loosely in rib pattern.

Left Front

Reattach yarn. Bind off 5 sts in the center for back neck. Continue on remaining 13(15) sts.

ROW 41 TO 70 (45 TO 78): K1, *P1, K1; rep from * to end.

ROW 71(79): K1, *P1, K1; rep from * to end.

ROW 72(80): P1, *K1, P1; rep from * to end.

ROW 73(81) TO 80(88): Rep ROW 71(79) AND 72(80).

Bind off loosely in rib pattern.

CONTINUES

SUPER
CROPPED
CARDIGAN

Sleeves

Join FRONT and BACK together at side seams. To find shoulder line, fold the sweater in half placing FRONT on top of BACK, and place markers on outside edges of shoulder line. Count down 29(31) rows from shoulder marker on each side for armhole openings, and place markers. Join side seams together below markers.

With circular needles, pick up 29(31) sts (1 st every other row) evenly spaced around each armhole (15[16] on FRONT and 14[15] on BACK) starting at underarm area and working clockwise. Join yarn to work in the rnd. Place marker.

RND 1 TO 15 (ODD ROWS): K1, *P1, K1; rep from * to end.

RND 2 TO 14 (EVEN ROWS): P1, *K1, P1; rep from * to end.

RND 16: *K2TOG, P2TOG; rep from * until 5(3) sts remain, K2TOG, P3TOG(P1) [14(16) sts remain].

RND 17 TO 25: *K1, P1; rep from * to end.

Bind off loosely in rib pattern.

Finishing

See finishing instructions on page 173.

HER CARDIGAN

SIZE

One size

FINISHED MEASUREMENTS

Chest (side seam to side
    seam): 25 inches
    (63.5 cm)

Length: 27 inches (69 cm)

LEVEL OF EXPERIENCE

Intermediate (time to
    complete: 8 to 16
    hours)

MATERIALS

Merino No. 5 by Loopy
    Mango, 5.3 ounce
    (150 g) balls each
    74 yards (68 m)

8 balls in Lady Blue

US size 19 (15 mm)
    needles, at least
    32 inches (80 cm) long

GAUGE

4 sts = 3 inches (7.5 cm)

4 rows = 2 inches (5 cm)

TIP

For less dramatic sleeves,
    pick up 4 fewer stitches
    at the armholes.

Just like the Her Turtleneck (see page 88), this cardigan is designed with coziness in mind. It is one of the most useful and versatile pieces; you can wear it from fall to spring and every time you put it on, you will look and feel effortlessly chic and comfortable. The back and fronts of this cardigan are basically just rectangles, so it's as easy as making a scarf.

Back

Cast on 38 sts.

ROW 1: K2, *P2, K2; rep from * to end.

ROW 2: P2, *K2, P2; rep from * to end.

ROW 3 TO 10: Rep ROW 1 AND 2.

ROW 11: K to end.

ROW 12: P to end.

ROW 13 TO 50: Rep ROW 11 AND 12.

ROW 51 TO 66: K to end.

Do NOT bind off.

Right Front

ROW 67: K16; turn work, leaving remaining sts on the needle or on a piece of waste yarn.

ROW 68 TO 82: K16.

ROW 83: K16.

ROW 84: P16.

ROW 85 TO 122: Rep ROW 83 AND 84.

ROW 123: K3, P2, K2, P2, K2, P2, K3.

ROW 124: P3, K2, P2, K2, P2, K2, P3.

ROW 125 TO 132: Rep ROW 123 AND 124.

Bind off in rib pattern.

CONTINUES

INTERMEDIATE

Left Front

Reattach yarn. Bind off 6 sts from the center for neck opening, then continue to work on the remaining 16 stitches for Left Front:

ROW 67 TO 82: K16.

ROW 83: K16.

ROW 84: P16.

ROW 85 TO 122: Rep ROW 83 AND 84.

ROW 123: K3, P2, K2, P2, K2, P2, K3.

ROW 124: P3, K2, P2, K2, P2, K2, P3.

ROW 125 TO 132: Rep ROW 123 AND 124.

Bind off loosely in rib pattern.

Sleeves

Place a marker on each side seam 32 rows up. Sew up both side seams. With circular needles, pick up 32 sts around armhole and join to work in the rnd.

RND 1 TO 29: K32.

RND 30: *K2TOG, P2TOG; rep from * to end of rnd (total 16 sts).

RND 31 TO 33: *K1, P1; rep from * to end of rnd.

Bind off loosely in rib pattern.

Finishing

NECKBAND

Pick up 93 sts evenly from RIGHT FRONT, neck, and LEFT FRONT edges.

ROW 1: K1, *P1, K1; rep from * to end.

ROW 2: P1, *K1, P1; rep from * to end.

ROW 3 AND 4: Rep ROW 1 AND 2.

Bind off loosely in rib pattern.

See additional finishing instructions on page 173.

URBAN
COWBOY
JACKET

One size

FINISHED MEASUREMENTS

Chest (side seam to side seam): 28 inches (71 cm)

Length: 23 inches (58 cm)

LEVEL OF EXPERIENCE

Intermediate (time to complete: 10 to 12 hours)

MATERIALS

Merino No. 5 by Loopy Mango, 5.3 ounce (150 g) balls each 74 yards (68 m)

8 balls in Polar Bear

US size 19 (15 mm) circular needles, at least 32 inches (80 cm) long

GAUGE

4 sts = 3 inches (7.5 cm)

4 rows = 2 inches (5 cm)

This is the jacket version of Urban Cowboy sweater style. I wanted to create something that was more festive than a basic sweater—and who doesn't like some fringe!

Back

Cast on 39 sts.

ROW 1: K1, *P1, K1; rep from * to end.

ROW 2: P1, *K1, P1; rep from * to end.

ROW 3 TO 10: Rep ROW 1 AND 2.

ROW 11 TO 15: K39.

ROW 16: P39.

ROW 17 TO 21: K39.

ROW 22: P39.

ROW 23 TO 27: K39.

ROW 28: P39.

ROW 29 TO 33: K39.

ROW 34: P39.

ROW 35: K39.

ROW 36: P39.

ROW 37 TO 41: K39.

ROW 42: P39.

ROW 43: K39.

ROW 44: P39.

ROW 45 TO 49: K39.

ROW 50: P39.

ROW 51: K39.

ROW 52: P39.

ROW 53 TO 57: K39.

ROW 58: P39.

ROW 59 TO 60: K39.

Right Front

SHAPE NECK

ROW 61: K18; turn work, leaving remaining sts on the needle or on a piece of waste yarn.

ROW 62 AND 63: K18.

ROW 64: P18.

ROW 65: K18.

ROW 66: P18.

ROW 67 TO 71: K18.

ROW 72: P18.

ROW 73: K18.

ROW 74: P18.

ROW 75: K18.

ROW 76: P18.

ROW 77 TO 81: K18.

ROW 82, 84, 86 (EVEN ROWS): P18.

ROW 83, 85, 87 (ODD ROWS): K18.

ROW 88 TO 91: K18.

ROW 92: P18.

ROW 93 TO 97: K18.

ROW 98: P18.

ROW 99: K18.

ROW 100: P18.

ROW 101 TO 105: K18.

ROW 106: P18.

ROW 107 TO 110: K18.

ROW 111 TO 120: *P1, K1; rep from * to end.

Bind off loosely in rib pattern.

CONTINUES

Left Front

SHAPE NECK

Reattach yarn and bind off 3 sts.

Work same as for RIGHT FRONT up to ROW 110.

ROW 111 TO 120: *K1, P1; rep from * to end.

Bind off loosely in rib pattern.

Sleeves

Join FRONT and BACK together at side seams. To find shoulder line, fold the sweater in half placing FRONT on top of BACK, and place markers on outside edges of shoulder line. Count down 32 rows from shoulder on each side for armhole openings, and place markers. Join side seams together below markers.

With circular needles, pick up 32 sts (1 st every other row) evenly spaced around each armhole (16 sts each on FRONT and BACK) starting at underarm area and working clockwise. Join yarn to work in the rnd.

RND 1: K32.

RND 2: P32.

RND 3: K32.

RND 4: P32.

RND 5 TO 9: K32.

RND 10: P32.

RND 11: K32.

RND 12: P32.

RND 13 TO 19: K32.

RND 20, 22, 24, 26, 28, 30: P32.

RND 21, 23, 25, 27, 29: K32.

RND 31: *K2TOG, P2TOG; rep from * to end.

RND 32 TO 34: *K1, P1; rep from * to end.

Bind off loosely in rib pattern.

Finishing

NECKBAND

Pick up 75 sts evenly from RIGHT FRONT, neck, and LEFT FRONT edges.

ROW 1: P1, *K1, P1; rep from * to end.

ROW 2: K1, *P1, K1; rep from * to end.

ROW 3: P1, *K1, P1; rep from * to end.

Bind off loosely in rib pattern.

See additional finishing instructions on page 173.

MAKE FRINGE

Cut 65 to 70 pieces of yarn, each 12 inches (30.5 cm) long. Fold each piece in half to make a loop. Attach to sweater by pushing the loop ends through the sweater from the front and bringing the free ends back though the loop. Tighten fringe by pulling on the ends. (See page 171.)

Evenly space the fringe in 2 rows along the BACK of the sweater.

PONCHO

FINISHED MEASUREMENTS

S/M

Chest (side seam to side
    seam): 29 inches (74 cm)

Length: 28 inches (71 cm)

M/L

Chest (side seam to side
    seam): 32 inches
    (81.5 cm)

Length: 30 inches (76 cm)

LEVEL OF EXPERIENCE

Intermediate (time to
    complete: 8 to 12 hours)

MATERIALS

Merino No. 5 by Loopy
    Mango, 5.3 ounce
    (150 g) balls each
    74 yards (68 m)

6(7) balls in Iceberg

US size 36 (20 mm), or size
    35 (19 mm) circular
    needles, at least
    24 inches (60 cm) long

GAUGE

5 sts = 4 inches (10 cm)

5 rows = 3 inches (7.5 cm)

The Poncho is a perfect piece to wear when seasons change, and
I wanted to design one that was super easy to make and to wear.

Front

Cast on 39(43) sts.

ROW 1: K1, *P1, K1; rep from * to
    end.

ROW 2: P1, *K1, P1; rep from * to
    end.

ROW 3 TO 12(14): Rep ROW 1 AND 2
    (working in rib st).

ROW 13(15): K39(43).

ROW 14(16): P39(43).

ROW 15(17) TO 54(56): Rep ROW
    13(15) AND 14(16) (working in
    St st).

Bind off loosely in rib stitch.

Back

Make same as for FRONT.

Finishing

Join FRONT and BACK together
    at shoulder and side seams. For
    shoulders, count 11 sts in from
    each side seam on FRONT and
    BACK on each shoulder, leaving
    remaining sts for neck opening,
    and place markers. Join the
    shoulders together along edges
    to marker.

ARMBANDS

With circular needles, pick up 32
    sts (1 st every other row) evenly
    around each armhole (16 sts each
    on FRONT and BACK) starting
    at underarm area and working
    clockwise. Join yarn to work in the
    rnd. Place marker.

RND 1 AND 2: *K1, P1; rep from * to
    end.

Bind off loosely in rib pattern.

NECKBAND

With circular needles, pick up 32 sts
    evenly around neckline, working
    clockwise (16 from front panel
    and 16 from back panel). Join to
    work neckband in the rnd. Place
    marker.

RND 1 TO 12: *K1, P1; rep from * to
    end of rnd.

Bind off loosely in rib pattern.

See additional finishing instructions
    on page 173.

S/M, M/L

FINISHED MEASUREMENTS

S/M

Chest side seam to side
seam: 27 inches (68 cm)

Length shoulder to hem:
25 inches (63 cm)

M/L

Chest side seam to side
seam: 30 inches (76 cm)

Length: 28 inches (71 cm)

LEVEL OF EXPERIENCE

Intermediate (time to
complete: 8 to 16 hours)

MATERIALS

Merino No. 5 by Loopy
Mango, 5.3 ounce
(150 g) balls each
74 yards (68 m)

9(11) balls in Spicy Hot Pink

US size 19 (15 mm) circular
needles, at least
32 inches (80 cm) long

GAUGE

4 sts = 3 inches (7.5 cm)

4 rows = 2 inches (5 cm)

Once in a while, I have this urge to abandon everything and live in a cabin in the woods as a recluse. If it ever happens, this will be the cardigan that I will bring with me. I would wear it when I walk in the woods with my dog; I would wear it when I read a book; I would wear it when I stare at the stars in the sky.

Back

Cast on 38(42) sts.

ROW 1: K2, *P2, K2; rep from * to end.

ROW 2: P2, *K2, P2; rep from * to end.

ROW 3 TO 10: Rep ROW 1 and 2.

ROW 11: K1, M1, K36(40), M1, K1

ROW 12: P40(44).

ROW 13: K1, M1, K38(42), M1, K1.

ROW 14: P42(46).

ROW 15: K42(46).

ROW 16: P42(46).

ROW 17 TO 60(66): Rep ROW 15 AND 16.

Right Front

SHAPE NECK

ROW 61(67): K18(20); turn work, leaving remaining sts on the needle or on a piece of waste yarn.

ROW 62(68): P18(20).

ROW 63(69) TO 106(118): Rep ROW 61(67) AND 62(68).

ROW 107(119): K2TOG, K16(18).

ROW 108(120): P17(19).

ROW 109(121): K2TOG, K15(17).

ROW 110(122): P16(18).

ROW 111(123): *P2, K2; rep from * to end (K2, *P2, K2; rep from * to end).

ROW 112(124): *P2, K2; rep from * to end (P2, *K2, P2, rep from * to end).

ROW 113(125) TO 120(132): Rep ROW 111(123) AND 112(124).

Bind off loosely in rib pattern.

CONTINUES

INTERMEDIATE

125

Left Front

Reattach yarn. Bind off 6 sts in the center for back neck. (You should have 18[20] sts left on the needles.)

ROW 61(67): K18(20).

ROW 62(68): P18(20).

ROW 63(69) TO 106(118): Rep ROW 61(67) AND 62(68).

ROW 107(119): K16(18), K2TOG.

ROW 108(120): P17(19).

ROW 109(121): K15(17), K2TOG.

ROW 110(122): P16(18).

ROW 111(123): *K2, P2; rep from * to end (K2, *P2, K2; rep from * to end).

ROW 112(124): *K2, P2; rep from * to end (P2, *K2, P2; rep from * to end).

ROW 113(125) TO 120(132): Rep ROW 111(123) AND 112(124).

Bind off loosely in rib pattern.

Sleeves

Join FRONT and BACK together at side seams. To find shoulder line, fold the sweater in half placing FRONT on top of BACK, and place markers on outside edges of shoulder line. Count down 32(36) rows from shoulder marker on each side for armhole openings, and place markers. Join side seams together below markers.

With circular needles, pick up 32(36) sts (1 st every other row) evenly spaced around each armhole (16[18] sts each on FRONT and BACK) starting at underarm area and working clockwise. Join yarn to work in the rnd. Place marker.

RND 1 TO 34: K32(36).

RND 35: *K2TOG, P2TOG; rep from * to end.

RND 36 TO 40: *K1, P1; rep from * to end.

Bind off loosely in rib pattern.

CONTINUES

Finishing

NECK AND FRONT BANDS

Pick up 90(100) sts evenly from
RIGHT FRONT, neck, and LEFT
FRONT edges.

ROW 1 TO 16(18): K90(100).

Bind off loosely in pattern.

POCKETS

Pick up 11 sts along each FRONT,
working from right to left 6 inches
(15 cm) in from front edge and
right above the rib.

ROW 1: P11.

ROW 2: K11.

ROWS 3 TO 8: Rep ROW 1 and
ROW 2.

ROW 9: P1, *K1, P1; rep from *
to end.

ROW 10: K1, *P1, K1; rep from *
to end.

ROWS 11 & 12: Rep ROW 9 and
ROW 10.

Bind off in Rib. Attach
Pockets to FRONTS at
Pocket side edge.

See additional finishing instructions
on page 173.

INTERMEDIATE

S/M, M/L

FINISHED MEASUREMENTS

S/M

Chest (side seam to side seam): 24 inches (61 cm)

Length: 22 inches (56 cm)

M/L

Chest: 27 inches (69 cm)

Length: 24 inches (61 cm)

LEVEL OF EXPERIENCE

Intermediate (time to complete: 5 to 8 hours for S/M and 7 to 9 hours for M/L)

MATERIALS

Merino No. 5 by Loopy Mango, 5.3 ounce (150 g) balls each 74 yards (68 m)

5(6) balls in Bubble Gum

US size 19 (15 mm) needles, at least 32 inches (80 cm) long

2 toggle buttons (optional)

GAUGE

10 sts = 7 inches (18 cm)

10 rows = 4 inches (10 cm)

This vest is worked in a seed stitch pattern—alternating knit and purl stitches, then purling the knits and knitting the purls on the following rows. You can make it with or without pockets, and the buttons are optional too. With chunky wool and toggle buttons, you don't need to worry about making buttonholes as the buttons can slip easily through a stitch. This is a great layering piece that can be warn all year round—over a dress or a tank top in summer or over a turtleneck and jeans in winter.

Back

Cast on 33(37) sts.

ROW 1, 3, 5: K1, *P1, K1; rep from * to end.

ROW 2, 4, 6: P1, *K1, P1; rep from * to end.

ROW 7 TO 56(60): K1, *P1, K1; rep from * to end (working in seed st).

Do NOT bind off.

Right Front

ROW 57(61): K1, *P1, K1; rep from * to last 18(20) sts, turn the work, leaving remaining sts on the needle or on a piece of waste yarn.

ROWS 58(62) TO 106(114): K1, *P1, K1; rep from * to end.

ROWS 107(115) TO 111(119) (ODD ROWS): K1, *P1, K1; rep from * to end.

ROWS 108(116) TO 112(120) (EVEN ROWS): P1, *K1, P1; rep from * to end.

Bind off loosely in rib pattern.

Left Front

Reattach yarn. Bind off 3 sts in the center for back neck. (You should have 15[17] sts left on the needles.)

ROW 57(61): K1, *P1, K1; rep from * to end.

ROWS 58(62) TO 106(114): K1, *P1, K1; rep from * to end.

ROWS 107(115) TO 111(119) (ODD ROWS): K1, *P1, K1; rep from * to end.

ROWS 108(116) TO 112(120 (EVEN ROWS): P1, *K1, P1; rep from * to end.

Bind off loosely in rib pattern.

CONTINUES

EVERYDAY
VEST

Finishing

Join FRONT and BACK together at side seams. To find shoulder line, fold the sweater in half, placing FRONT on top of BACK, and place markers on outside edges of shoulder line. Count down 32 rows from shoulder marker on each side for armhole openings, and place markers. Join side seams together below markers.

ARMHOLE BANDS

With circular needles, pick up 30(32) sts (1 st every other row) evenly around each armhole (15 [16] sts each on FRONT and BACK) starting at underarm area and working clockwise. Join yarn to work in the rnd. Place marker.

RND 1 AND 2: *K1, P1; rep from * to end.

Bind off loosely.

FRONT BANDS AND NECKBAND

Pick up 89(93) sts evenly from RIGHT FRONT, neck, and LEFT FRONT edges.

ROW 1, 3: K1, *P1, K1; rep from * to end.

ROW 2: P1, *K1, P1; rep from * to end.

Bind off loosely in rib pattern.

See additional finishing instructions on page 173.

POCKET

On each FRONT, pick up 9(11) sts on the rows 5 (6) up from the bottom of vest and 4 (5) in from side seam. Work pocket as follows:

ROW 1 TO 11: K1, *P1, K1; rep from * to end.

ROW 12: P1, *K1, P1; rep from * to end.

ROW 13: K1, *P1, K1; rep from * to end.

Bind off in rib.

Sew pockets at side edges to FRONTS.

Using same yarn, attach buttons (if using).

LOOPY THE LOOP VEST

SIZE

One size

FINISHED MEASUREMENTS

Chest (side seam to side seam): 19 inches (48 cm)

Length: 28 inches (71 cm)

LEVEL OF EXPERIENCE

Intermediate (time to complete: 12 to 16 hours)

MATERIALS

Merino No. 5 by Loopy Mango, 5.3 ounce (150 g) balls each 74 yards (68 m)

7 balls total: 4 Col A= Polar Bear, 2 Col B = Sunshine, 1 Col C = Bubble Gum

US size 35 (19 mm) circular needles, at least 24 inches (60 cm) long

GAUGE

7 sts = 4 inches (10 cm)

7 rows = 3 inches (8 cm)

Outside diameter of loop stitch = 1" (2.5 cm)

Please note: If your loop stitch is more than 1" (2.5 cm), you could run out of yarn.

ABBREVIATIONS USED

ML – Make Loop (see pages 164–165)

If you want to learn a new stitch, I highly recommend loop stitch. It's so much fun! You can create playful texture with it for any garment. This vest is definitely a statement piece. To tone it down, pair it with some jeans and a T-shirt. If you are not into color blocking, you can make it all in one color.

Back

With Col A, cast on 33 sts.

Foundation row: K33.

ROW 1: *K1, ML; rep from * until 1 st remains, K1.

ROW 2: K to end.

ROW 3: K2, *ML, K1; rep from * until 3 sts remain, ML, K2.

ROW 4: K to end.

ROW 5 TO 24: Rep Row 1 to 4.

ROW 25 TO 44: With Col B, rep ROW 1 TO 4.

ROW 45 TO 68: With Col A, rep ROW 1 TO 4.

ROW 69 TO 80: With Col C, rep ROW 1 TO 4.

Right Front

Continue working on the first 13 sts. The remaining sts can stay on the needle or on a piece of waste yarn.

ROW 81 TO 92: With Col C, rep Row 1 to 4.

ROW 93 TO 116: With Col A, rep Row 1 to 4.

ROW 117 TO 136: With Col B, rep Row 1 to 4.

ROW 137 TO 160: With Col A, rep Row 1 to 4.

Bind off loosely.

Left Front

With Col C, reattach yarn. Bind off 7 sts in the center for back neck.

ROW 81 TO 92: Rep ROW 1 TO 4.

ROW 93 TO 116: With Col A, rep ROW 1 TO 4.

ROW 117 TO 136: With Col B, rep ROW 1 TO 4.

ROW 137 TO 160: With Col A, rep ROW 1 TO 4.

Bind off loosely.

Finishing

Seam sides, leaving armholes of 13 inches (33 cm).

See additional finishing instructions on page 173.

CONTINUES

One size

FINISHED MEASUREMENTS

Chest (side seam to side
    seam): 24 inches
    (61 cm)

Length: 38 inches
    (96.5 cm)

LEVEL OF EXPERIENCE

Intermediate (time to
    complete: 10 to 13
    hours)

MATERIALS

Merino No. 5 by Loopy
    Mango 5.3 ounce
    (150 g) balls each
    74 yards (68 m)

9 balls in Dorian Gray

US size 19 (15 mm) circular
    needles, at least 32
    inches (80 cm) long

GAUGE

4 sts = 3 inches (7.5 cm)

4 rows = 2 inches (5 cm)

I love sweater coats—they are so cozy. I wanted to design a piece that I can throw on over a pair of jeans, a dress, or even just a slip and feel as if I have a snuggly blanket wrapped around me.

Back

Cast on 37 sts.

ROW 1: K1, *P1, K1; rep from * to end.

ROW 2: P1, *K1, P1; rep from * to end.

ROW 3 TO 10: Rep ROW 1 AND 2.

ROW 11: K37.

ROW 12: P37.

ROW 13: K37.

ROW 14: P37.

ROW 15 TO 66: Rep ROW 13 AND 14.

ROW 67 TO 82: K37.

Do NOT bind off.

Right Front

SHAPE NECK

ROW 83 TO 98: K16 sts; turn work, leaving remaining sts on the needle or on a piece of waste yarn.

ROW 99: K16.

ROW 100: P16.

ROW 101 TO 154: Rep ROW 99 AND 100.

ROW 155 TO 164: *P1, K1; rep from * to end.

Bind off loosely in rib pattern.

Left Front

SHAPE NECK

Reattach yarn. Bind off 5 sts from the center for back neck.

ROW 83 TO 98: K16.

ROW 99: K16.

ROW 100: P16.

ROW 101 TO 154: Rep ROW 99 AND 100.

ROW 155 TO 164: *P1, K1; rep from * to end.

Bind off loosely in rib pattern.

CONTINUES

Sleeves

Join FRONT and BACK together at side seams. To find shoulder line, fold the sweater in half placing FRONT on top of BACK, and place markers on outside edges of shoulder line. Count down 36 rows from shoulder marker on each side for armhole openings, and place markers. Join side seams together below markers.

With circular needles, pick up 36 sts (1 st every other row) evenly spaced around each armhole (18 sts each on FRONT and BACK), starting at underarm area and working clockwise. Join yarn to work in the rnd. Place marker.

RND 1 TO 30: K36.

RND 31: *K2TOG, P2TOG; rep from * to end (total 18 sts).

RND 32 AND 33: *K1, P1; rep from * to end.

Bind off loosely in rib pattern.

Finishing

FRONT AND NECK BANDS

Pick up 129 sts evenly from RIGHT FRONT, neck, and LEFT FRONT edges.

ROW 1 AND 3: K1, *P1, K1; rep from * to end.

ROW 2: P1, *K1, P1; rep from * to end.

Bind off loosely in rib pattern.

See additional finishing instructions on page 173.

INTERMEDIATE

NEW YORKER
LONG VEST

One size

Chest (side seam to side
    seam): 21 inches (53 cm)

Length: 38 inches (96.5 cm)

Intermediate (time to
    complete: 4 to 8 hours)

Big Loop by Loopy Mango,
    40 ounce (1,100 g) balls
    each 125 yards (115 m)

2 skeins in Oatmeal

US size 50 (25 mm) circular
    needles, at least 32
    inches (80 cm) long

US size S (19 mm) or U
    (25 mm) crochet hook
    (optional)

Toggle button (optional)

2 sts = 3 inches (7.5 cm)

1 row = 1 inch (2.5 cm)

I have always loved wearing vests. A vest is a great item to have in your wardrobe, because you can layer it in so many different ways, especially between seasons. You can put it on over a T-shirt, turtleneck, or dress. It will cozy you up and make you look effortlessly chic.

Back

Cast on 17 sts.

ROW 1: K1, *P1, K1; rep from * to end.

ROW 2: P1, *K1, P1; rep from * to end.

ROW 3: K17.

ROW 4: P17.

ROW 5 TO 38: Rep ROWS 3 AND 4.

Do not bind off.

Right Front

SHAPE NECK
ROW 39: K8; turn work, leaving remaining sts on the needle or on a piece of waste yarn.

ROW 40: P8.

ROW 41 TO 74: Rep ROWS 39 AND 40.

ROWS 75 TO 76: *P1, K1; rep from * to end.

Bind off loosely in rib pattern.

Left Front

Reattach yarn. Bind off 1 st in the center back.

ROW 39: K8.

ROW 40: P8.

ROW 41 TO 74: Rep ROW 39 AND 40.

ROW 75 TO 76: *K1, P1; rep from * to end.

Bind off loosely in rib pattern.

CONTINUES

Finishing

POCKETS

Pick up 5 sts along each FRONT, working from right to left, 3 inches (7.5 cm) in from front edge and 15 inches (38 cm) in from lower edge.

ROW 1: P5.

ROW 2: K5.

ROW 3 TO 6: Rep ROWS 1 AND 2.

Bind off.

Join Pockets to FRONTS at Pocket side edges.

See additional finishing instructions on page 173.

BELT

With your fingers or large crochet hook, make a chain to desired length for the belt (see page 174). Attach toggle button if using.

Everyone has their favorite coat. This one is my favorite, and that's why I named it this way. Big Loop is the best choice for knitting a blanket, because of its softness and thickness. But you can't wear a blanket. I always feel cold and always want to wrap myself in one, and when I wear this coat, I feel as if I'm wrapped up in a giant wool blanket.

SIZE

S/M

Note: Due to the rich fibers used, this coat is on the heavier side. A M/L size would make this too heavy to wear, and therefore we do not advise this.

FINISHED MEASUREMENTS

Chest (side seam to side seam): 21 inches (53 cm)

Length: 40 inches (101.5 cm)

LEVEL OF EXPERIENCE

Intermediate (time to complete: 6 to 8 hours)

MATERIALS

Big Loop by Loopy Mango, 40 ounce (1,100 g) skeins each 120 yards (110 m)

2 skeins in Ivory

US size 50 (25 mm) circular needles at least 32 inches (80 cm) long

GAUGE

2 sts = 3 inches (7.5 cm)

1 row = 1 inch (2.5 cm)

TIPS

We recommend knitting tighter for this project—this way the jacket won't stretch out as much when worn.

Back

Cast on 15 sts.

ROW 1 AND 3: K1, *P1, K1; rep from * to end.

ROW 2 AND 4: P1, *K1, P1; rep from * to end.

ROW 5: K15.

ROW 6: P15.

ROW 7 TO 42: Rep ROW 5 AND 6.

Right Front

SHAPE NECK

ROW 43: K5; turn work, leaving remaining sts on the needle or on a piece of waste yarn.

ROW 44: P5.

ROW 45: K5.

ROW 46: P5.

ROW 47 TO 80: Rep ROW 45 AND 46.

ROW 81 AND 83: K1, *P1, K1; rep from * to end.

ROW 82 AND 84: P1, *K1, P1; rep from * to end.

Bind off.

Left Front

Reattach yarn. Bind off 5 sts in the center for back neck.

ROW 43: K5.

ROW 44 TO 84: Rep same as for RIGHT FRONT.

Bind off.

Sleeves

Join FRONT and BACK together at side seams. To find shoulder line, fold the sweater in half placing FRONT on top of BACK, and place markers on outside edges of shoulder line. Count down 12 rows from shoulder marker on each side for armhole openings, and place markers. Join side seams together below markers.

With circular needles, pick up 12 sts (1 st every other row) evenly spaced around each armhole (6 sts each on FRONT and BACK) starting at underarm area and working clockwise. Join yarn to work in the rnd. Place marker.

RND 1 TO 14: K12.

RND 15: *K2TOG, P2TOG; rep from * to end (total 6 sts).

RND 16 AND 17: *K1, P1; rep from * to end.

Bind off.

CONTINUES

Finishing

BACK NECK AND FRONT BANDS
Working clockwise, evenly pick up
a total of 56 sts: 25 sts along
RIGHT FRONT edge, 6 sts along
BACK Neck edge, and 25 sts
along LEFT FRONT edge.

ROW 1 TO 3: K56.

Bind off.

POCKETS
Cast on 5 sts for each pocket.

ROW 1 AND 3: K1, *P1, K1; rep from
* to end.

ROW 2 AND 4: P1, *K1, P1; rep from
* to end.

ROW 5 AND 6: K5.

Bind off.

Sew the pockets, 15 inches (38 cm)
up from bottom edge, and 4 inches
(10 cm) in from front edge.

See additional finishing instructions
on page 173.

STITCHES
&
TECHNIQUES

HOW TO WORK INCREASES

To increase means knitting a stitch in such a way that you end up with two stitches knitted from one. There are several methods used to increase stitches. Usually the pattern will specify which method is to be used.

KFB: Knit in front and back

One of the most common methods is Knit in Front and Back (KFB). It means that you insert the needle in the usual way from front to back (same as regular knit stitch) (A), wrap the yarn around the needle (B), and pull it through (C). But instead of releasing the stitch, you reinsert the needle through the back of the same stitch (D), wrap the yarn around (E), pull it through (F), and then release (G). You now will have two stitches.

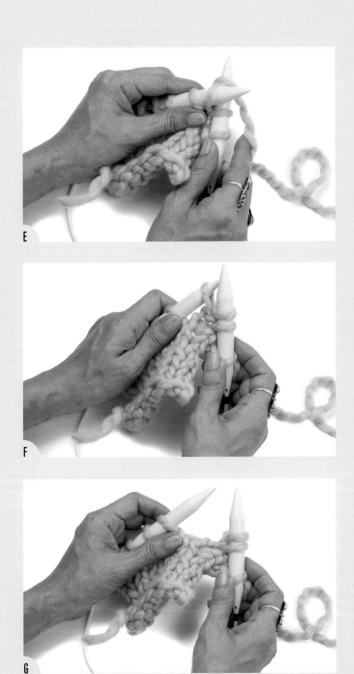

E

F

G

M1: Make One

One of the ways to increase stitches in knitting is called Make One, or M1.

Find a horizontal strand of yarn between two stitches.

A Pick it up and place it on the left needle.

B/C Use the right needle to knit through the back of that loop.

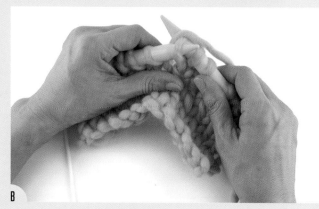

A

B

C

D

HOW TO WORK DECREASES

K2TOG: Knit 2 together

To decrease means knitting (or purling) two (or more) stitches together to reduce the number of stitches in a row. There are several methods to decrease stitches. One of the common decreases is knitting 2 stitches together.

A Insert the needle in the usual way from front to back (same as a regular knit stitch), but instead of inserting it through one stitch, insert it through two stitches together from the left needle.

B Wrap the yarn around the right-hand needle (toward you)—yarn over.

C Pull the yarn through the loop.

D Take the stitch off the left needle.

STITCHES
&
TECHNIQUES

GARTER STITCH

When knitting a flat piece (scarf, blanket, etc.), the garter stitch is achieved by knitting every row or purling every row.

When knitting in the round with a circular needle (beanie, sleeve, cowl, etc.), the garter stitch is achieved by alternating knit and purl rounds.

STOCKINETTE OR STOCKING STITCH

When knitting a flat piece (scarf, blanket, etc.), stockinette stitch is achieved by alternating knit and purl rows.

When knitting in the round (beanie, sleeve, cowl, etc.), stockinette stitch is achieved by knitting every round.

A Right side (RS)

B Wrong side (WS)

B

B

RIB STITCH

Rib stitch is achieved by alternating knit and purl stitches on one row, then knitting the knit stitch and purling the purl stitch on the next row. For example, a 1 × 1 rib means that you knit one stitch, purl one stitch, and then repeat until the end of the row. On your second row, you knit the knits and purl the purls.

Example of 1 × 1 Rib

Cast on 5 sts.

ROW 1: K1, *P1, K1; rep from * to end.

ROW 2: P1, *K1, P1; rep from * to end.

You can also work wider ribs, like 2 × 2 ribs.

SEED OR MOSS STITCH

Seed stitch is achieved by alternating knit and purl stitches and then knitting the purl stitch and purling the knit stitch on following rows.

Example

Cast on 5 sts.

ROW 1: K1, *P1, K1; rep from * to end.

ROW 2: Rep ROW 1.

FISHERMAN RIB STITCH

Fisherman rib is different from traditional rib in the way this stitch is knit and in its look. It looks thicker and more three-dimensional, and it feels squishier compared to regular rib. But it uses more yarn. This stitch uses K1B, P1B, or both, depending on the pattern.

Example

Cast on 6 sts.

ROW 1: Purl all sts in the row.

ROW 2: *P1, K1B; rep from * to end.

ROW 3: Rep ROW 2.

See pages 160–161 for K1B and P1B.

Tip

It is a good exercise to experiment with different tensions. It is important to confirm that your tension is correct by making a swatch before starting a project.

GAUGE

Gauge refers to the number of stitches and rows in a given measurement.

> XX stitches (sts) = XX inches (XX cm)
>
> XX rows = XX inches (XX cm)

Needle size affects your gauge. For example, using a smaller-size needle with the same yarn will make the stitches tighter than using a larger-size needle.

YARN TENSION

Tension refers to how tightly you hold or pull the yarn when knitting. If you are a tight knitter, it means that you have a tendency to pull the yarn tightly and the garment you are knitting will come out smaller in size, since every stitch will take up less space. If you are a loose knitter, it means that you have a tendency to not pull the yarn very tightly, and the garment will come out bigger in size. Or you could be in between. Some people can control their tension so that they can knit tightly, loosely, or in-between.

FLAT KNITTING

Flat knitting is knitting a flat piece of fabric, such as a scarf, a blanket, or a panel in a sweater or cardigan. There are two sides to flat knitting. One is called the "right side," which is often abbreviated as "RS." The other one is the "wrong side," abbreviated as "WS." The right side is the face of the fabric. This is the side that will be on the outside of the garment. The wrong side is the back side of the fabric and will be on the inside of the garment. When you are facing the right side of the garment, you are working on a right-side row. When you are facing the wrong side of the fabric, you are working on a wrong-side row.

CIRCULAR KNITTING, OR KNITTING IN THE ROUND

Circular knitting, or knitting in the round, is the method used when the fabric is worked so that it creates a seamless tube such as a hat, a cowl, or a sleeve. When you knit circularly, the stitches are cast on and the circle of stitches is joined together. Circular knitting is worked in rounds (the equivalent of rows in flat knitting). You can only work this method using circular needles or double-pointed needles, not straight needles (double-pointed needles are beyond the scope of this book). When knitting in the round, you are always working on the right side of the fabric.

Tips

When connecting the first round, it is very important not to twist stitches by accident.

Use a stitch marker or a piece of yarn tied in a loop at the start of every round.

HOW TO JOIN TWO ENDS OF YARN TOGETHER

There are many different ways to join two ends of yarn, but we are only going to cover methods that are relevant to the yarns used in this book.

When joining two ends of a bulky, natural-fiber wool yarn, like Big Loop or Merino No. 5, the best method is to use a felting needle and pad to felt the strands together—this way you can make a completely seamless connection. Hold two ends of yarn together and poke them with a felting needle multiple times—make sure to insert the needle through both strands.

You can also simply knot two ends of yarn together (the knot will be somewhat visible) and then weave the ends of the yarn back into the garment or trim the yarn.

Or you can sew the two ends together with sewing thread and a regular sewing needle, using a thread color that closely matches the color of yarn. This is also suggested for yarns made with synthetic fibers or superwash wool, as they will not felt.

With Mohair So Soft or any similar fuzzy yarn, you can just knot the two ends together, as a knot will be almost invisible due to the fuzziness of the yarn. You can also felt the ends, as on page 158.

K1B: KNIT 1 BELOW

A Insert your working needle
   (in right hand) into the space
   below the stitch on your needle
   (left hand), as shown.

B Work a knit stitch.

C Pull the worked stitch, with the
   stitch on top, off the needle.

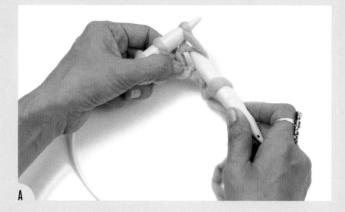

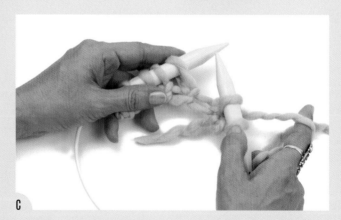

P1B: PURL 1 BELOW

A Insert your working needle (in right hand) into the stitch below the stitch on your needle (left hand).

B Work a purl stitch.

C Pull the worked stitch, with the stitch on top, off the needle.

CABLES

There are many different ways to work cables. These are just some of them.

T3F: Twist 3 Front

A Slip two stitches onto cable needle and hold them in front of the work.

B Purl next stitch from left needle.

C Knit two stitches from cable needle.

Note: For T3B (Twist 3 Back) slip next stitch onto cable needle and hold at back of work, knit next 2 stitches from left-handed needle, then purl stitch from cable needle.

A

B

C

C4B: Cable 4 back

A Slip two stitches onto cable needle and hold them in back of the work.

B Knit next two stitches from left needle.

C Knit two stitches from cable needle.

Note: C4F is worked the same way as C4B, except instead of holding the stitches on the cable needle in back, you hold them in front.

ML:
MAKE LOOP

A Insert needle as if to knit.

B Yarn over and hold the yarn with your left thumb.

C Pass the yarn in between the needles, behind the right-hand needle.

D Move the loop from left thumb to right thumb.

E Slip the stitch as if to purl.

F Pull the first stitch over the second stitch.

G You now have a loop stitch on the right-hand needle.

ASTER FLOWER STITCH

Slip the first stitch.

A Insert the needle as if to knit through next stitch and wrap the yarn around right needle two times.

B Pull it through the loop and finish the knit stitch.

C Repeat five times.

D Slip the next stitch.

Repeat steps A–D until end of row.

E

F

G

Slip first stitch in the next row.

E Slip next five stitches to right needle, dropping extra loops.

F Slip these five stitches back to left needle.

G P1, yo, P1, yo, P1. Work all 5 stitches together without removing them from the needle (you will end with five stitches on the right needle). Slip next stitch.

Repeat steps E–G until end of row.

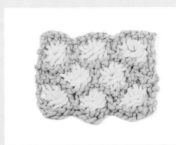

Front and back of Aster Flower motif

PICKING UP STITCHES FOR A SLEEVE

For cardigans, vests, or jackets, find the middle—for example, if the total number of rows for the body of this project is 120, your middle would be Row 60. For sweaters, start at the shoulder. Count the same number of stitches on each panel, counting every other row (not every row). For example, if you need to pick up a total of 24 stitches, count 12 stitches on the front panel and 12 stitches on the back panel. Use a stitch marker to mark your last stitch (in the underarm area). It is helpful to seam the shoulder first. Starting from the last stitch in the underarm area on the front panel and with the right side of the work facing you, insert the needle into the stitch, wrap the yarn around the needle, and pull the yarn through the stitch. Work your way around clockwise until you reach the stitch marker again. Think of it as your cast-on round.

JOINING SIDE AND SHOULDER SEAMS

"Joining side seams" (A) is used for sweaters, cardigans, and jackets, and "joining shoulder seams" (B) is used for sweaters.

Attach yarn to one end of a piece and, using a tapestry needle or your fingers, weave the yarn back and forth across the opening, inserting the needle through each stitch on opposite panels.

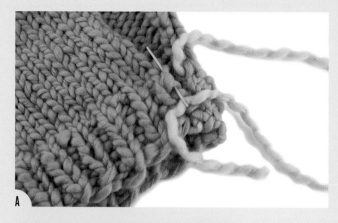

A

ATTACHING FRINGE

Cut pieces of fringe two times the desired length of fringe.

A Fold each piece of yarn in half.

B Insert the folded yarn through the stitch where you would like the fringe to go.

C Pull it through.

Tip

A crochet hook can be handy to attach fringe, especially if your garment requires a lot of it.

B

C

POMPOM

Cut a piece of cardboard to measure 4 × 6 inches (10 × 15 cm.)

Using the short end of the cardboard, wrap yarn around the cardboard 30 to 50 times.

Carefully pull cardboard out and tie a 15-inch- (38-cm-) long piece of yarn firmly around the middle of the bundle to secure.

Cut the loops along the opposite untied edge with scissors. Fluff yarn.

Trim pompom, making sure not to cut the tie you used to secure the middle.

FINISHING

Weaving in Yarn Ends

When you are finished knitting your project, you will need to do one more step—weave in all loose ends. You only need a tail of about 1–2 inches (2–4 cm). Push it inside the garment and simply hide it in between the stitches. You can use a large tapestry needle (A) or your fingers to weave in the ends and secure them with a felting needle (B), or sew them with a sewing needle and thread in a matching color.

Blocking

If you are an experienced knitter, you are probably familiar with blocking. Simply put, blocking is a process of reshaping a knitted garment. None of the projects in this book require blocking. It is simply not necessary or even practical when knitting with such bulky yarns.

CROCHET STITCHES

Ch: Chain Stitch

A   Make a slip knot.

B   Insert the crochet hook through the slip knot.

C   Wrap the yarn around the hook in a clockwise direction.

D   Pull yarn through the loop.

A

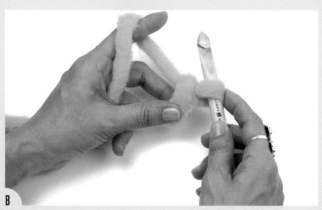

B

C

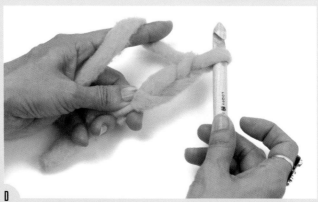

D

A

Ss (or Sl st): Slip Stitch

A Insert the crochet hook from front to back into the required stitch.

B Wrap the yarn around the hook in a clockwise direction.

C Pull yarn through both the work and (D) the loop on the hook.

B

C

D

My mom taught me how to knit and crochet at a young age, but, as with many young people, I didn't fully appreciate the beauty of handcrafts at the time. And while I don't have a formal education in fashion or design, I have always been interested in fashion. Loopy Mango designs are inspired by everything around me—nature, art, fashion, vintage knitwear. I love going to flea markets and vintage stores, and I collect vintage textiles. It is somewhat of an addiction, and an interest I'm happy to have grown and expanded on over the years.

And I am attracted to the tactile experience of working with natural fibers. The entire process from sourcing fiber to developing colors, spinning it into yarn, designing, and hand knitting each piece is an elaborate but ultimately immensely gratifying process. My goal in creating pieces has always been to maximize the beauty of natural fibers to ensure that the end result is something that can be appreciated by those who share my aesthetic.

LOOPY MANGO FLAGSHIP STORE

Beacon, New York, is the new home of the Loopy Mango store and show-room. It is a charming little town located in the Hudson Valley, accessible from New York's Grand Central Terminal, an easy and beautiful train ride with breathtaking views of the Hudson River. Beacon is also home to a contemporary art museum, Dia:Beacon, that occupies a former Nabisco box printing factory—a gorgeous space with more than 34,000 square feet of skylights, considered a model of early-twentieth-century industrial architecture.

Loopy Mango's store is located at 500 Main Street and is a destination for knitters from all over the world. It showcases all Loopy Mango products—DIY kits, yarns, knitting needles, and crochet hooks. A variety of knitted garments from all collections are available for trying on. Knowledgeable and friendly staff will get you started on a knitting project in no time. Beginner-friendly knitting classes and workshops are offered weekly and are prefect for a day-trip visitor—learn how to knit in just two hours, and in some classes complete an entire project too! Loopy Mango's motto is: Anyone can be creative, all you have to do is give it a try.

RESOURCES

If you like to learn from a video, the @loopymango channel on YouTube has a variety of video lessons to help you follow along with all of the techniques described in this book.

DIY KITS

There are many do-it-yourself (DIY) kits on the market. A kit is great for a beginner, as it usually has everything you need to complete a project. Typically a DIY kit will include yarn, knitting needles, and instructions. A knitting level will also be specified. Loopy Mango offers DIY kits for all of the projects in this book. Some of them are available in a box, which makes a great gift for a knitter or an aspiring knitter. Some kits will come with online video tutorials too.

For Loopy Mango and other chunky yarns and large knitting tools, visit these stores.

CANADA

The Knit Cafe Toronto, Toronto, ON:
   theknitcafetoronto.com

The Knitting Loft, North York, ON:
   theknittingloft.ca

Stash Needle Art Lounge, Calgary, AB:
   stashlounge.com

Statement Junkie, Sherwood, AB::
   statementjunkie.com

CHINA

Blue Balloon, Ningbo City, Zhejiang:
   bfyarn.taobao.com

Fireweed Parade, Chengdu, Sichuan:
   shop242348422.world.taobao.com

Lotus Yarns, Xingtai, Hebei
   lotusyarns.com

JAPAN

Amirisu, Kyoto City: shop.amirisu.com

KOREA, SOUTH

Playwool, Seoul: playwool.com

POLAND

Czac Zamotac, Krakow: czaszamotac.pl

UNITED KINGDOM

Liberty, London: libertylondon.com

Love Crafts: lovecrafts.com

UNITED STATES

ARKANSAS:

Arkansas Yarn Co., Malvern:
   arkansasyarnco.com

CALIFORNIA:

A Verb for Keeping Warm, Oakland:
   averbforkeepingwarm.com

Cast Away, Santa Rosa:
   castawayyarnshop.com

Little Knittery, Los Angeles:
   thelittleknittery.com

Sheared Sheep, Newport Beach:
   shearedsheep.godaddysites.com

Wildfiber Studio, Santa Monica:
   wildfiberstudio.com

COLORADO:

Lula Faye Fiber, Boulder: lulafayefiber.com

Fancy Tiger, Denver: fancytigercrafts.com

CONNECTICUT:

Twist Yarn Shoppe, Niantic:
   twistyarnshoppe.com

Westport Yarns, Westport:
   westportyarns.com

FLORIDA:

Four Purls Yarn Shop, Winter Haven:
   fourpurls.com

Sheep Thrills, Lauderhill:
   sheepthrillsknitting.com

LOUISIANA:

The Quarter Stitch, New Orleans:
   quarterstitch.com

MARYLAND:

Knits and Pieces, Annapolis:
knitsandpiecesofannapolis.com

MASSACHUSETTS:

Adventures in Knitting, Harwich:
adventuresinknitting.com

Bead and Fiber, Boston: beadandfiber.com

Gather Here, Cambridge:
gatherhereonline.com

Knotty Knit, South Dartmouth: knottyknit.com

MINNESOTA:

StevenBe, Minneapolis: stevenbe.com

MISSOURI:

Unwind Fiber Arts, Lee's Summit:
unwindfiberarts.com

MONTANA:

The Farmer's Daughter Fibers, Great Falls:
thefarmersdaughterfibers.com

Stix Yarn, Bozeman: stixyarn.com

Yarn Bar, Billings: yarn.bar

NEW JERSEY:

Balzac Fibers, Ocean Grove: balzacfibers.com

Grace & Purl, Avon-by-the-Sea:
graceandpurl.com

Wool & Grace, Summit: woolandgrace.com
theknittingcup.com

NEW YORK:

Brooklyn General Store, Brooklyn:
brooklyngeneral.com

Downtown Yarns, New York:
downtownyarns.com

Knitting Nation, Nyack:
knittingnation.com

Loopy Mango, Rhinebeck: loopymango.com

The Knitting Room, Windham:
theknittingroomny.com

Observatory, Hastings on Hudson:
theobservatoryshop.com

OHIO:

Sew to Speak, Columbus:
sewtospeakshoppe.com

Yarn It & Haberdashery, Columbus:
yarnitanddash.com

OREGON:

Close Knit, Portland: closeknitportland.com

PENNSYLVANIA:

Wild Hand, Philadelphia: wild-hand.com

RHODE ISLAND:

Mermaid's Purl, Wickford:
themermaidspurl.com

TEXAS:

The Knitting Cup, Georgetown:
theknittingcup.com

The Modern Skein, Montgomery:
themodernskein.com

VIRGINIA:

Fibre Space, Alexandria: fibrespace.com
theknittingcup.com

Finch Knitting + Sewing Studio,
finchknittingsewingstudio.com

WYOMING:

Knit on Pearl, Jackson: www.knitonpearl.com

RESOURCES

ACKNOWLEDGMENTS

First and foremost I would like to thank Anna, my business partner and best friend. Without her, none of this would be possible. I know how blessed I am to have a friend and business partner like her. She works tirelessly to make it possible for me to have creative freedom and space. Ever since we first met, she saw something in me and has given me endless support and love. For that I am forever grateful.

I would like to thank my mom, who taught me how to knit, and my sister, Hechong, who is the harshest critic of them all. It's because of her brutal honesty that with each collection I can push myself and my creativity further.

I would like to thank every member of our Loopy Mango team for their hard work every single day and for helping me make my vision a reality.

INDEX

Editor: Meredith A. Clark
Designer: Deb Wood
Production Manager:
    Kathleen Gaffney

Library of Congress Control
Number: 2018958321

ISBN: 978-1-4197-3808-1
eISBN: 978-1-68335-669-1

Printed and bound in China

10 9 8 7 6 5 4 3 2

Abrams books are available
at special discounts when
purchased in quantity for
premiums and promotions
as well as fundraising or
educational use. Special
editions can also be created to
specification. For details, contact
specialsales@abramsbooks.com
or the address below.

Abrams® is a registered
trademark of Harry N. Abrams, Inc.

ABRAMS The Art of Books
195 Broadway, New York, NY 10007
abramsbooks.com